# A CLASS DIVIDED
*THEN AND NOW*

# WILLIAM PETERS

# A CLASS DIVIDED

## *THEN AND NOW*

*Expanded Edition*

*With a foreword by*
KENNETH B. CLARK

YALE UNIVERSITY PRESS
NEW HAVEN AND LONDON

Printed in the United States of America by
BookCrafters, Inc., Chelsea, Michigan.

International standard book numbers: 0–300–03666–3 (cloth)

0–300–04048–2 (pbk.)

Library of Congress catalog card number: 87–50411

The paper in this book meets the guidelines for permanence and
durability of the Committee on Production Guidelines for Book
Longevity of the Council on Library Resources.

10 9 8 7 6 5 4 3

For Jane Elliott and her third-grade class
of 1970:

| | | |
|---|---|---|
| John Benttine | Tammy Bill | Verla Buls |
| Sandra Dohlman | Susan Ginder | Raymond Hansen |
| Greg Johanns | Rex Kozak | Laurie Mayer |
| Donna Reddel | Russell Ring | Brian Saltou |
| Sheila Schaefer | Julie Smith | Roy Wilson |
| | Milton Wolthoff | |

# FOREWORD

"You have to be taught to hate" was once a fashionable phrase. It seemed to be a key to how to protect American children from the virus of racial prejudice. It follows from this thinking that if children are not taught to reject others or to accept discrimination directed against others who differ from themselves in such superficial characteristics as skin color, then they will be free of the social and psychological burdens of racism. The educational implication of this optimistic perspective is that children can be taught to develop and express sensitive concerns for the hopes, anxieties, and humanity of others. This would be an important contribution to the success of the civil rights movement.

Unfortunately, it has become increasingly clear that in a society in which racism is pervasive, it is easier to teach children prejudices than to teach sensitivity for other human

1

beings. One would have expected that after the U.S. Supreme Court stated in its historic *Brown* decision of May 1954 that racially segregated schools violated the equal protection clause of the United States Constitution, and psychologically damaged the victims of such organized racism, educational institutions would be in the forefront, leading American children away from racism. However, this was not to be. The resistance of many public officials, school boards, parents, and educators to effective desegregation of our public schools revealed the depth and extent of racism in American society. The fact that desegregated schools could provide an opportunity for educators to teach children to accept others and to understand the commonality of their fellow human beings was denied by the persistence of racism. Rather, the continued racial organization of public schools made this critical educational institution a vehicle for the perpetuation of racism and the damaging of human beings. While educators for the most part did not directly teach our children to be cruel to others who differed in skin color, their silence and rationalizations made them accessories to the continued hostilities of children who were taught by their parents to resist school desegregation.

The evidence from Jane Elliott's "discrimination day" experiment and William Peters' documentation of the results in his book *A*

*Class Divided, Then and Now* are most significant in demonstrating that it is possible to
counter the teaching of hatred by having children experience and understand the deep hurt
inevitably associated with discrimination and
rejection by others. This understanding came
as a result of requiring the children to experience rejection themselves, a necessary first
step, it seems, in communicating this type of
human sensitivity. It took a great deal of courage and commitment for Jane Elliott, the
teacher, to assume the risks of even temporary
trauma to her students and of stated or unstated
resentment on the part of parents and fellow
teachers. But the results and follow-up appear
to have justified these risks.

A most notable finding from this social experiment was that the positive influence on
these children was not temporary. Jane Elliott
and William Peters had the fortunate opportunity to meet with the former students and
discuss their values and perspectives fourteen
years after the original experience. These former students revealed that their attitudes, sensitivity, and social maturity remained intact.
Even though they experienced this type of dis-
turbing role-playing as third-graders for only a
few days and direct or indirect negative racial
attitudes and counterforces were a continuing
part of their environment, having experienced
personal hurt and rejection continued to have
a positive effect on their ability to empathize

3

with others. This demonstration of the resilience of normal human beings indicates that it is possible for social institutions, particularly schools, to educate children away from hatred and cruelty toward others. It is also significant that in developing positive attitudes and self-esteem, the children were able to demonstrate positive academic achievement. They not only developed respect for others, they also expressed a dynamic self-respect.

Jane Elliott's replication of the experiment with adult employees of the Iowa Department of Corrections leaves a number of questions that should be pursued. The employees were subjected to a clearly artificial situation for a half-day. They were not subjected to the authority of a teacher. In spite of these facts, their reactions were not unlike those of the third-graders. Those who were told they were inferior resented being discriminated against. Those who were told that they were superior and given privileges relished even this temporary and artificial status. It is not known to what extent this short training session influenced their racial attitudes.

Jane Elliott's work with young children, the follow-up, and the training sessions with adults demonstrate that it is possible for schools—educational and social institutions—to socialize and educate normal human beings away from racial hostilities and rejection. With understanding and commitment, it is possible to develop and implement a sequential educational program that can contribute to the attainment of this humane goal. Freeing human beings from the burdens of rejection and cruelty directed toward others and freeing the victims from the consequences of hatred and rejection are most important goals for education. Educators who are concerned and mature enough to share these goals with Jane Elliott and William Peters can develop a systematic educational program toward the attainment of genuine human values:

• In their training and preparation, teachers can and must be taught the foundations, significance, and educational value of human and race relations. It is not enough that teachers be certified in terms of their mastery of subject matter and teaching methods. They must also understand the relationship between cognitive skills and human understanding and acceptance. They must be able to communicate and teach these humane values to their students not only by their words but also by their actions.

• The Jane Elliott experiment and methods could be modified for use at various educational levels—elementary, middle, and high schools.

• Subject matter and disciplines in colleges and specialization in professional schools could be taught as an integral part of human sensitivity.

A major, an inescapable goal of educational institutions is to broaden the perspective of human beings—to develop a truly functional empathy—to free human beings from the constrictions of ignorance, superstition, hostility, and other forms of inhumanity. Jane Elliott's contribution, as described in William Peters' *A Class Divided, Then and Now* demonstrates that it is possible to educate and produce a class of human beings united by understanding, acceptance, and empathy.

KENNETH B. CLARK

# AUTHOR'S NOTE

This new edition of *A Class Divided* is a continuation of the edition originally published in 1971. It contains the complete, unrevised text of the first edition (Chapters I–IX). The material that follows, beginning with Chapter X (page 105), is new.

I am grateful to the American Broadcasting Company and to Yale University Films for permission to make use of material gathered while producing television documentaries on the subject of this book.

Video cassettes and 16mm film prints of the 1970 ABC News documentary *The Eye of the Storm* are available from Guidance Associates, The Center for Humanities, Communications Park, Box 3000, Mount Kisco, New York 10549 (800–431–1242). Video cassettes and 16mm film prints of the 1985 Public Broadcasting System *Frontline* documentary *A Class Divided* are available from PBS Video, 1320 Braddock Place, Alexandria, Virginia 22314–1698 (800–344–3337).

*New Haven, Connecticut*      *William Peters*

A CLASS DIVIDED
*THEN AND NOW*

# I

On any normal weekday morning, Jane Elliott looked forward to getting to her classroom at the Riceville, Iowa, Community Elementary School and to the teaching job she loved. Eager to pick up the threads of the previous day's lessons, delighting in her third-graders' sense of wonder at anything new, she saw each day as a kind of adventure in the company of children she enjoyed. Often she was reluctant, when the day was over, to see them leave. Not infrequently, they felt the same way. Once they had seriously proposed that the entire class spend the night at school.

But that Friday in April, 1968, was not a normal morning. The day before, Martin Luther King had been murdered in Memphis. For Jane, that had suddenly made a lot of things different. She had made a decision about what she would do in her class, a decision that now

11

made her reluctant to leave the house for school.

Her husband, Darald, was perfectly capable of seeing that their four children were properly fed and dressed for school before he left for his own job. He did it often when she had a particular reason for getting to the school a little early. Yet today she fussed about the kitchen, urging one child to eat and another to change his shoes, sipping at a second cup of coffee—knowing that she was only stalling.

Finally, with a glance at her watch, she shrugged into a jacket and said good-by. Darald, who knew what she was planning winked at her and then smiled encouragingly. She grimaced at him as she went out the door.

She had made her decision, and she would stick to it, though she dreaded what she felt sure lay ahead. For a while, at least, she would be making each of her twenty-eight students unhappy; for a time, all would dislike her and resent what she was putting them through. She had worked hard since September to establish a warm and trusting relationship with each of them, and she had been proud of their success as a class in becoming a happy, co-operative, productive group. What she was now going to do would strain those hard-won ties, perhaps even threaten them. It was hardly a pleasant prospect.

Still, driving her car through the quiet, early-morning streets, she refused to give in to her

growing sense of apprehension. She had to do
something if she was any kind of teacher at all.
She refused to do something that was essen-
tially meaningless. What she had thought of
promised at least a chance of being an effective
lesson. Nor was there time now to plan anything else. Whatever was to be done would
have to be done today, while the shock of Dr.
King's brutal assassination still reverberated in
the mind.

She had made her decision in horror and
anger and shame the night before as she sat
on the living-room floor ironing the stitched
sheets of an Indian tepee and watching the television coverage of the aftermath of the murder.
That decision had stood the test of the
dawn's colder appraisal, and she was not going
to permit a faint heart to change it.

The things she had planned to teach inside
the giant tepee would now have to wait, she
decided, for all of them had paled beside the
urgent message that had burst from her television set the night before. Now, the senseless-
ness, the irrationality, the brutality of race
hatred cried out to be explained, understood,
committed irrevocably to memory in a lesson
that would become a part of the life of each
child she could reach with it.

That was what she had struggled half the
night to devise; it was what she had finally
thought of: a lesson that might accomplish just
that. She knew that her children would ask

about the murder, that they had undoubtedly watched what she had watched. They had already discussed Martin Luther King in class. Now they would have to discuss his violent death. But this time, they would do more than that. Much more.

Setting aside her doubts, she opened the door of Room 10, turned on the lights, and went to her desk. As she sat down, she saw before her the Sioux prayer she had planned to teach the children after they had erected the giant tepee: "Oh, Great Spirit, keep me from ever judging a man until I have walked a mile in his moccasins." It was precisely the lesson she hoped to teach today, though not at all in the way she had contemplated. First, she thought unhappily, they are going to have to walk that mile.

It began, really, even before the bell rang. A boy came into the room bursting with the news. "They shot that King yesterday!" he said excitedly. "Why did they shoot that King?"

"We'll talk about that," Jane promised, and after the opening exercises, they did. When everyone had had a chance to tell what he knew, Jane asked them what they had heard and what they knew about Negroes. In the tiny town of Riceville, population 898, and the sparsely settled farming area surrounding it, there were no Negroes. In the school's textbooks, like those in so many American schools, Negroes were neither mentioned nor pictured.

Whatever her children said, then, Jane assumed would have come from parents, relatives, and friends, from what they had learned in school —in her own class and in the grades before— and from things they had seen and heard in a rare movie or on the radio or television.

Rather quickly, a pattern developed from their answers. Negroes weren't as smart as white people. They weren't as clean. They fought a lot. Sometimes they rioted. They weren't as civilized. They smelled bad.

None of it was said in a vicious way. There was no venom, no fear, no hate, but rather a sort of disapproval, a sense of disdain. Some of the children quoted parents to back up points, though there was no real argument. It was as though their teacher had asked them to describe a vaguely unpleasant experience they had all shared. They told what they knew about Negroes calmly, reaching back in their memories for details, corroborating each other, expanding on each other's points. Behind her expression of friendly interest, Jane was appalled.

She asked them to define the words "prejudice," "discrimination," "race," "inferior." That was not difficult; they had discussed these concepts before. Then they talked about some of the things Negroes in various parts of the United States were not permitted to do. Finally, Jane asked them if they could imagine how it would feel to be a black boy or girl.

"This they discussed at some length," Jane

Elliott says now, "and eventually, they decided that they could. Now, in spite of the things they had 'known' about Negroes, they became sympathetic. They felt sorry for black children; they didn't think it was fair for them to be treated differently. And they had had enough of the subject. Dr. King's death had been adequately disposed of. I could easily have stopped right there.

"Yet all I could think of as I saw this attitude of sympathetic indifference develop was the way I had myself reacted to racial discrimination all these many years: Sure, an incident can anger you. Sure, you feel sorry about the way blacks are being treated. Sure, something ought to be done about it. And now, what shall we talk about?"

But Jane Elliott's identification with the children in her class went deeper. Raised, like them, on a farm near Riceville, growing up in the all-white, all-Christian community, she had herself lived in the midst of the kinds of prejudices they had expressed in their descriptions of Negroes. Though she had long since rejected those prejudices, there was still much that she could see of herself as a child in the children who sat now at their desks in front of her. She had once been there, too, and was now, at the age of thirty-five, looking back through all the years that had intervened. What she saw—even in her own strong, yet inactive, opposition to racism—was simply not enough.

"I felt desperately," she says, "that there had to be a way to do more as a teacher than simply tell children that racial prejudice is irrational, that racial discrimination is wrong. We've all been told those things. We know them, at least in the sense that we mouth them at appropriate times. Yet we continue to discriminate, or to tolerate it in others, or to do nothing to stop it. What I had racked my brain to think of the night before was a way of letting my children find out for themselves, personally, deeply, what discrimination was really like, how it felt, what it could do to you. Now the time had come to try it."

What happened next in Jane Elliott's classroom was, as far as she knew, a product of her own mind. She had never heard of anyone else who had done it. She was not even sure it was a good idea. She knew only that she had to do something, and this was all she had thought of to try.

The idea went back to a half-angry, half-humorous remark she had made to a college roommate years before. Returning to school after a weekend in Riceville, she had told her roommate about an argument she had had with her father on the subject of race. Remembering as she talked about it how her father's hazel eyes had blazed at her accusations of prejudice, she told her roommate, "If hazel eyes ever go out of style, my father's going to be in trouble."

She had no sooner said it than it struck both girls as an interesting observation. Skin color, eye color, hair color or texture: it made as much sense, they decided, to discriminate on the basis of one as another. The two of them talked far into the night about how it must feel to be a Negro in America.

Jane Elliott never forgot that discussion. Later, when she and Darald were married and he became the assistant manager of a supermarket in the Negro section of Waterloo, Iowa, she saw his Negro customers and employees as different from herself only in this: they knew, as she didn't, how it felt to be the object of prejudice, hate, and fear. Everything else she learned about Negroes convinced her that they were basically no different than whites.

Then, with Darald suddenly transferred to another city, Jane had been faced with the problem of renting their house. A real estate agent and neighbors cautioned her not to rent to blacks. She paid little attention until a woman telephoned in response to an ad. "She asked if the house was for whites or colored," Jane says, "and suddenly those warnings sprang into my mind. I hesitated a moment and then said that all of my neighbors were white. She said, 'Oh, well, thank you anyway,' and hung up, and I stood there with the telephone in my hand feeling as though I had defected to the enemy.

"For a long time after that, I felt like a snake.

18

I knew what I should have done—I should have said the neighborhood was white but that she could come and look at the house if she were interested. But, of course, I hadn't. I tried to analyze why I had evaded the issue, and I was forced to the conclusion that I had backed away from my principles out of fear of my neighbors' opinions. If we had rented to a Negro family and later wanted to move back, we would have had to face their anger. I saw that when the chips were down, I had not been able to face that. And I hated myself for it."

It was after that experience that Jane began to read about the racial crisis in America. One of the books she read was John Howard Griffin's *Black Like Me*, the story of a white man's experiences in the South with his skin dyed a deep brown. Here was a man who had found out what it was like to be a Negro, and Jane suffered with him the thousand daily insults, the inconveniences, the fears, the wounds to pride that Southern Negroes experience in the course of simply going about the business of living.

Then, suddenly, on the night of the day that Martin Luther King was murdered, all of these memories and experiences had coalesced into an idea of how she might give her third-graders a sense of what prejudice and discrimination really meant.

Jane took a deep breath and plunged in. "I

don't think we really know what it would be like to be a black child, do you?" she asked her class. "I mean it would be hard to know, really, unless we actually experienced discrimination ourselves, wouldn't it?" Without real interest, the class agreed. "Well, would you like to find out?"

The children's puzzlement was plain on their faces until she spelled out what she meant. "Suppose we divided the class into blue-eyed and brown-eyed people," she said. "Suppose that for the rest of today the blue-eyed people became the inferior group. Then, on Monday, we could reverse it so that the brown-eyed children were inferior. Wouldn't that give us a better understanding of what discrimination means?"

Now there was enthusiasm in their response. To some, it may have meant escape from the ordinary routine of a school day. To others, it undoubtedly sounded like a game. "Would you like to try that?" Jane asked. There was an immediate chorus of assent.

# II

Divided by eye color, Jane Elliott's class was made up of seventeen children with blue eyes, three with green eyes, eight with brown eyes. To make the groups more even, the green-eyed children were lumped with the brown-eyed. Because those with blue eyes still outnumbered the others—and because Jane's bright blue eyes might tend to make things a little easier for them—she had decided that they should represent the minority group the first day.

"Today," she told the class, "the blue-eyed people will be on the bottom and the brown-eyed people on the top." At their puzzled looks, she went on. "What I mean is that brown-eyed people are better than blue-eyed people. They are cleaner than blue-eyed people. They are more civilized than blue-eyed people. And they are smarter than blue-eyed people."

When they still looked puzzled, Jane nodded shortly. "It's true. It really is."

Now the brown-eyed children began to look at each other in wonder. They sat up straighter in their chairs, waiting to hear more. The blue-eyed children frowned, stirred uneasily, not understanding. One blue-eyed boy slumped way down in his chair. "What color are your eyes?" Jane asked him.

"Blue," the boy said, straightening up.

"Is that the way we've been taught to sit in class?"

"No," the boy said.

"Do blue-eyed people remember what they've been taught?" Jane asked the class. There was a chorus of "No's" from the brown-eyed children as they began to see how it would work. The blue-eyed boy now sat bolt upright, his hands folded neatly in the exact center of his desk. A brown-eyed boy near him, one of his close friends in the room, gave him a withering, disdainful look. It began that quickly.

The rules for the day were enumerated to the growing delight of the brown-eyed children and the increasing discomfort of the blue-eyed. Brown-eyed children could use the drinking fountain in the room as usual. Blue-eyed children were to use paper cups. The brown-eyed children would have five extra minutes of recess. They would go first to lunch, could choose their lunch-line partners, and could go back for seconds. The blue-eyed children could do none of these things.

"Who should sit in the front of the room?" Jane asked.

"The brown eyes!" shouted the brown eyes.

"Who should be our row leaders?"

"The brown eyes!" they shouted again.

At her nod of approval, there was a great tumult of sound and motion as the children pushed their desks and chairs to the new positions.

The blue-eyed children winced and squirmed as the list of rules grew longer. "Blue-eyed people are not allowed to play with brown-eyed people unless they are invited," Jane told them. "They may not play on the big playground equipment at recess. And they may not take the small playground equipment out of the room."

With the rules established, Jane swung quickly into the day's regular schoolwork. When a brown-eyed child stumbled in reading aloud, she helped him. When a blue-eyed child stumbled, she shook her head and called on a brown-eyed child to read the passage correctly. When a blue-eyed boy, tense and nervous, rolled a corner of a page of his reading book into a tight curl as he awaited his turn to read, Jane displayed the book to the class. "Do blue-eyed people take care of the things they are given?" she asked.

"No!" shouted the delighted brown-eyed children.

That was the way it went. The brown-eyed children took a special joy in baiting their blue-eyed classmates. None invited their erstwhile friends to play with them at recess. One lovely and brilliant blue-eyed girl, among the most popular children in the class, almost disintegrated under the pressure. She walked in a slouch, became suddenly awkward, tripped twice over things, did poorly in her work. At recess, walking disconsolately across the playground, she was struck across the back by the deliberately outstretched arm of a brown-eyed girl who the day before had been her best friend.

"You got in my way," challenged the brown-eyed girl, "and I'm better than you, so you have to apologize."

Abjectly, the blue-eyed girl mumbled an apology. The other girl walked away in triumph.

"Long before noon," Jane says now, "I was sick. I wished I had never started it. During the morning recess, I went to the teachers' lounge and told three other teachers what I was doing. They laughed. I went back to my empty room and cried.

"By the lunch hour, there was no need to think before identifying a child as blue or brown-eyed. I could tell simply by looking at them. The brown-eyed children were happy, alert, having the time of their lives. And they were doing far better work than they had ever done before. The blue-eyed children were miserable. Their posture, their expressions, their entire attitudes were those of defeat. Their classroom work regressed sharply from that of the day before. Inside of an hour or so, they looked and acted as though they were, in fact, inferior. It was shocking.

"But even more frightening was the way the brown-eyed children turned on their friends of the day before, the way they accepted almost immediately as true what had originally been described as an exercise. For there was no question, after an hour or so, that they actually believed they were superior. The fact that we were going to change roles on Monday was forgotten. Everything was forgotten in the face of the undeniable proof that the blue-eyed children were inferior to them. It was as though someone had pointed out to them something they simply had not noticed before. Weren't the blue-eyed children making more mistakes than they were? Of course. Wasn't the teacher finding fault almost exclusively with the blue-eyed children? Of course. Wasn't it clear that she liked the brown-eyed children better? Of course. What better proof did you need?

"Sometime that day, I pulled down a roller map at the front blackboard. As I let go, it flew back into its case with a great clatter. It was something I had done before. As I turned disgustedly to pull it down again, a brown-eyed girl in the front row said, 'Well, what do you expect? You've got blue eyes.'"

Startled, Jane recovered her composure before she turned back to the class. "Is that why I did that?" she asked. There were nods of agreement from several brown-eyed children. Then a blue-eyed boy came to her defense. "Naw," he said. "She's never been able to pull it down right."

That brought up the question of her status as a teacher, for if she had blue eyes and was, hence, inferior, how could she teach brown-eyed children? "I have a better education," she told them. "I've been to college. And even though I may not be as smart as brown-eyed people, I'm better educated than brown-eyed people who haven't been to college."

"That's right," said a brown-eyed boy. "She knows more than brown-eyed kids, but she's not as smart as the brown-eyed teachers in the school."

"Why do you think I'm just a teacher and not the principal of the school?" Jane asked, wondering just how far they would carry this line of reasoning.

"Because Mr. Brandmill has brown eyes!" cried a brown-eyed girl with pride. Dinsmore Brandmill was the school's principal.

Jane shrugged her shoulders in mute agreement, wondering now what color Mr. Brandmill's eyes really were.

# III

Before the end of school on Friday, Jane Elliott reminded the children of how the day had begun. "We decided to try this," she said, "to see if we could learn something about discrimination. And we said that on Monday, the brown-eyed people would be on the bottom and the blue-eyed people would be on top. We'll talk more about that on Monday, but I want to remind you that that's the way it's going to be."

Four hands shot up, and Jane called on a brown-eyed boy. "If you're going to do that, I'm not coming to school," he said. "Neither am I," said a brown-eyed girl. "Me neither," said another.

"How many of you think you're coming to school Monday?" Jane asked. All but the three who had spoken raised their hands, though other brown-eyed children were slow to respond. "All right. We'll see who's here on Monday." Then, turning back after a quick glance at the clock, Jane noticed the looks of pleasure at the promise of revenge on the faces of many of the blue-eyed children. "Do you blue-eyed people think you're going to enjoy Monday more than you did today?" she asked.

"Yes!" they shouted, laughing.

"Well, we'll see about that, too. But it's still Friday now, and it's time to go home. So get the things off your desks, and when the bell rings, the brown-eyed people may go first to their lockers and line up first for the buses. And remember, when you get on the buses, you blue-eyed people are to sit as far to the rear as you can." The bell rang as she finished, and in a few minutes, the school day was over. Jane, exhausted, sank into the chair at her desk in the empty classroom, trying desperately to sort out her impressions of what had happened, still horrified at much that she had seen, wishing once more that she had never started it, but knowing, with a sense of dread, that she would have to go through the whole thing again on Monday.

Over the weekend, she half-anticipated telephone calls from some of the parents or from Mr. Brandmill. No one telephoned. She told her mother and father what she had done, how the children had responded, and she could see that her father was shaken at the description of the

way the brown-eyed children had behaved toward their blue-eyed classmates.

"It was a lonely, scary weekend," she says. "I
talked and talked and talked about what had
happened, not only to my parents but to Darald
and my two sisters, who had been teachers. I
couldn't get it out of my mind. And I couldn't
help feeling very much alone. I had done this
on my own, and whatever happened, I was
solely responsible. At home, I caught myself
looking at my own four children, wondering
how I would feel if a teacher did to them what
I had done to my class. I thought I would approve, but I couldn't be sure. And then, suddenly, I found myself wondering if my children
would have behaved as my third-graders had.
I had no answer to that at all."

On Monday, all of the children in Jane's class
came to school. She made no mention of the
three who had said they wouldn't come. Briefly,
she recalled to them all what they had done on
Friday and how it had begun. Then, as the blue-
eyed children became restless and fidgety, she
said, "I lied to you on Friday. I told you brown-
eyed people are better than blue-eyed people.
That's not true."

There was an expectant hush. "The truth is
that blue-eyed people are better than brown-
eyed people. They are smarter than brown-
eyed people. They are . . ."

She guessed, as she went through the entire

list for the second time, that there might now be greater resistance to what she was saying. Perhaps, having been fooled once, they would simply have no more of this nonsense. Yet, watching their faces carefully, she saw that it was having an effect. The faces that had been gleeful on Friday were rapidly falling into depressed scowls. Those that had been glum on Friday brightened with pleasure. To make sure that she was getting through, she tossed off the names of famous people, asking, as though it were generally known, what color their eyes were. The blue-eyed children came through as expected. "Blue!" they cried happily with each new name.

As Jane continued reversing Friday's procedure, reviewing the restrictions that today would apply to the brown-eyed children, a number of blue-eyed boys and girls gloated visibly at the prospect of revenge. The changing of the seating was accomplished quickly, and the reminder signs that had been placed on the drinking fountain and paper cups were reversed. Almost at once, Jane began finding fault with brown-eyed children.

"I had not expected that the brown-eyed children, knowing full well after their experience on Friday that it was all an exercise and that it would last only a day, would react as intensely as the others had to the experience of discrimination," Jane says now. "But they did. Within minutes, they had become nervous, depressed, resentful. The only real difference that day was that the blue-eyed children, now on top, were noticeably less vicious in their treatment of the underlings than the latter had been to them.

"I speculated about the reason for this, but I could only guess why. Was it because a whole weekend had intervened? Was it because they were in the numerical majority even when they were being discriminated against and felt that there was somehow safety in numbers? Or was it just possibly because, having experienced discrimination themselves, they were able to identify with the 'inferior' group and felt sorry for them? Naturally, I hoped it was the last, though I couldn't be sure."

Toward the end of that day, Jane ended the exercise, telling the class that it had all been a lie. She asked them what they had learned and was heartened by their answers. "Does the color of your eyes have anything to do with what kind of person you are?" she asked.

They literally shouted their answer at her. "No!"

The tensions of the two-day exercise broke like a dam giving way to a flood, and she laughed with them, comforted those who cried with relief, and nearly cried herself at the sight of boys who had been separated by the color of their eyes wrestling happily together, of girls, eyes wet with joy, hugging friends they had thought forever lost.

On Tuesday, Jane led a wide-ranging discussion of what they had learned. There was little need to encourage the children to contribute; all were bursting with things to say. Finally, with the air completely cleared, Jane asked each child to write a composition defining "discrimination," describing how he had felt on each of the two days, and telling who Martin Luther King was. When the papers had been corrected for spelling and punctuation, they were read aloud to the group.

"Discrimination," Julie Kleckner wrote, "is being judged by the color of your skin or the color of your eyes or the church you go to." Carol Anderson wrote, "Discrimination is a word for when a person is judged not by what he does but by the color of his skin. I found out what it feels like in school." Dale Brunner put it more personally. "Discrimination," he wrote, "is happy and not happy."

Brown-eyed Sindee Hockens, having defined discrimination, went on to write: "Our room heard about it when Martin Luther King died and we wanted to see what it felt like to be a Negro child, with black skin. The brown-eyed children were the whites and blue-eyed children were the Negroes. This was Friday. I have brown eyes. I was happy. The brown-eyed children were hot-shots; I felt good inside.

"On Monday, I felt mad because I was being discriminated against. The blue-eyed people got to be first in line and the teacher just explained to the blue eyes their mistakes and bawled us brown eyes out. I was sick."

Debbie Anderson, also brown-eyed, said of Monday, "I felt mad and I wanted to tie the people with blue eyes up and quit school because they got to do everything first and we had to do everything last. I felt dirty. And I did not feel as smart as I did on Friday. Discrimination is no fun. Martin Luther King did not like discrimination against Negroes."

"On Monday," brown-eyed Dale Brunner wrote, "I could have locked them in jail because I was mad. The blue-eyes got to be first in the lunch line, and got to be first in lunch, and got five extra minutes of recess. I didn't want to work. I didn't feel like I was very big. Discrimination is no fun at all. I am glad I am not a Negro and being judged by my skin."

Theodore Perzynski described the two days: "On Friday, we practiced discrimination. The brown-eyed people got to do things first. I have blue eyes. I felt like slapping a brown-eyed person. It made me mad. Then I felt like kicking a brown-eyed person. I felt like quitting school. The brown-eyed people got five extra minutes of recess.

"On Monday I was happy. I felt big and smart. Then we got five extra minutes of recess. We got to do everything first. And we got to take out the playground equipment. I do not like discrimination. It makes me sad. I would not like to be angry all my life."

33

Dennis Runde, blue-eyed, wrote, first, of Friday: "The people with brown eyes could do almost anything. The people with blue eyes could not do half the things the people with brown eyes did. I felt left out because I have blue eyes. I felt like giving them all black eyes."

Of Monday, Dennis wrote: "On Monday, April 8, we had Discrimination Day again only the people with blue eyes got to be the wheels. Boy, was that fun! We got to do all the things first. That was living it up. I felt like I was smarter, bigger, better, and stronger."

Bruce Fox's contribution was succinct: "Discrimination is being judged by your skin color. On Friday, the people with brown eyes got to have a recess and art and I have brown eyes. I was happy. We did the same things on Monday except the people with blue eyes got to have long recess and p.e. [physical education] and I felt like blowing the teacher sky high."

Nor was there any question that the children knew who Martin Luther King was. "Martin Luther King wanted Negroes to have what they wanted just as white people do," Carol Anderson wrote. "And he was killed for doing this. He was killed by discrimination."

Billy Thompson wrote: "Martin Luther King died trying to save colored people from discrimination. White people at least could treat colored people like any other people."

# IV

When all the papers had been read, Jane recalled for her third-graders the things they had
said about Negroes before the exercise began:
that they weren't as smart, as clean, or as civilized as white people; that they fought and
rioted; that they smelled bad. Some of the
things they had written in their compositions
now came back to them with new force:

Debbie Anderson: "I felt dirty."

Sindee Hockens: "I was sick."

Dale Brunner: "I didn't feel like I was very
big."

Debbie Hughes: "I felt like quitting school."

Billy Thompson: "I felt like crying."

Dennis Runde: "I felt left out."

Theodore Perzynski: "I felt like kicking a
brown-eyed person."

Kim Reynolds: "I felt like being a drop-out."

One by one, the children examined what they

had felt to be true of Negroes in the light of their own experiences. Was it possible, Jane asked, that being accused of being careless almost from the day you were born might tend to make you something less than careful? Is being told again and again that you are not as clean as another person likely to give you a positive attitude toward cleanliness?

If you know that no matter how hard you work, you will be called dumb because your eyes are the wrong color, will that make you want to try your hardest and do your best work? If you feel angry or sick or left out because of discrimination against you in school, are you going to want to go to school? Is it easy to keep your mind on schoolwork when you know that others are looking down on you because of the color of your eyes?

Each question sparked a discussion; each discussion led further toward a conclusion. Discrimination not only hurt, it affected the way you behaved. The way you behaved affected not only the kind of work you did, it affected the way you felt about yourself. The way you behaved, the kind of work you did, and the way you felt about yourself—all these affected the way you appeared to other people; in fact, they could affect the way you actually were. Discrimination could change the kind of person you were if it went on long enough. And there was another conclusion: it was no better—and no more accurate—to judge a person by the color of his skin than by the color of his eyes. Neither told you anything important about the person.

"Before we were through," Jane says, "I was convinced that the children had learned a great deal from the exercise and that it was learning that would stick. And though there had been no thought on my part that the exercise was an experiment from which I might learn, I felt when it was over that I had learned more than the children had.

"I learned far more than I wanted to know about the effect of being considered superior and what reactions it could trigger in nice, average, middle-class, white American children. All of the children enjoyed being considered superior, and the feeling that they were had obviously pushed them to do better work than they had ever done before. But some of them took a savage delight in keeping the members of the 'inferior' group in their place, in asserting their 'superiority' in particularly nasty ways. I had not seen this side of my students before, nor was I really aware of its existence, at least in them. I was wholly unprepared for their lack of compassion for people they normally considered their best friends.

"I wasn't prepared, either, for the degree of anger and rebellion expressed by every child at becoming a second-class citizen. During our discussion on Tuesday, for example, it came out that there had been long, serious conversations

37

on the playground and in the boys' and girls' rooms about what the 'inferior' group would like to do to me. It ranged from throwing things at me to killing me. Nor had I realized until I saw it how destructive a feeling of inferiority really is, how it can literally change a personality, how it can drag down efficiency, destroy motivation.

"During those two days, the atmosphere in the classroom changed from one in which the children felt mutual respect and even admiration for each other to one in which the tension from feelings of contempt, greed, conceit, frustration, envy, and despair was almost unbearable. We were all glad it was over, but what we had seen of ourselves and each other, what we had felt either as 'superior' or 'inferior' people, what we had learned, not only intellectually but in a deeply emotional way as well—all these left their imprint on everyone in that classroom, students and teacher as well."

From the beginning, Jane had conceived of the exercise as a classroom lesson for her third grade and nothing else. Yet, as it proceeded—and particularly after it was over—she began to anticipate some kind of response from outside Room 10. What had happened was too explosive, too deeply moving for word of it not to reach someone who had not been there. The three teachers in the teachers' lounge had laughed that first day, but perhaps others, hearing about it, would at least want to know more.

She had expected that at least one parent might telephone, either to complain or to praise, and that if she did not hear about it directly, she would hear from Mr. Brandmill, the principal. None of these things happened. It was as though the entire exercise had been conducted in the strictest secrecy.

"When I told Mr. Brandmill what I had done," Jane says, "he expressed interest. When I described how the children had behaved, he was surprised. I had a feeling that he thought they had been pretending, acting out roles assigned to them by the teacher like good little boys and girls. It was then that I first realized how difficult it would be to make anyone believe what had actually happened. You almost had to *be* there, to see it as it was going on, to know that the children, far from acting, had somehow accepted the situation as real despite the fact that it had been presented to them as unreal."

With her father, Jane had greater success. Describing what had happened in great detail, she could see that he felt the children's wounded pride, their hurt feelings, their acceptance of an imposed status of inferiority as an almost personal blow. He was appalled at the behavior of the "superior" group. "Before this," Jane says, "my father, though he would never have hurt anyone, held many of the same beliefs about Negroes that my third-graders had expressed before the exercise. I could almost see those beliefs eroding in the days after the exercise as we discussed it again and again. It affected his views deeply."

When word of Jane's unique lesson in discrimination did finally get out, it was because of the admiration of a close friend of what she had done. Among the people her friend told was Merritt Messersmith, owner and publisher of the Riceville *Recorder,* a twelve-page weekly. Messersmith, fascinated, wanted to know more, and two weeks after the classroom exercise, he published a story, along with excerpts from some of the children's compositions.

If the *Recorder's* news story had an impact in Riceville, Jane Elliott did not feel it. Close friends, who had known what she had done, mentioned the story. Then she heard that it had been picked up by a wire service. That, Merritt Messersmith could not resist telling her with a certain pride. Then, finally, came a reaction, though not at all what Jane had expected. Johnny Carson telephoned and asked her to come to New York to appear on the "Tonight" show. "I didn't quite know what to make of that," Jane says, laughing, "but I went."

After her appearance, mail began to come in from all parts of the country. It continued, sporadically, throughout the summer. Most was favorable, though some was ugly. But the most interesting response for Jane came, finally, from the mother of one of the girls in her class, and it was not to the television show but to what had happened in the classroom.

They met by accident. The girl's mother said, "I want you to know that you've made a tremendous difference in our lives since your Discrimination Day exercise. My mother-in-law stays with us a lot, and she frequently uses the word 'nigger.' The very first time she did it after your lesson, my daughter went up to her and said, 'Grandma, we don't use that word in our house, and if you're going to say it, I'm going to leave until you go home.' We were delighted. I've been wanting to say that to her for a long, long time. And it worked, too. She's stopped saying it."

# V

When school began again in the fall, there
were in Jane Elliott's new third-grade class a
number of children who needed special help
in reading. Selected by their former second-
grade teachers as those in their classes who
were farthest behind in learning to read, these
children were, for the first time at the school,
placed as a group in a single third-grade classroom. Jane, after completing a course in remedial reading at Rochester, Minnesota, had volunteered to take them.

From the beginning, she made it a point to
talk frankly with these children about their
reading problems, to point out that they could
be solved, to convince them that they were not
dumb, as they might have thought or even been
told they were, and to promise them that, together, she and they would soon prove it. By
the middle of the year, they had.

But long before that, at the very beginning of the school year, Jane had tried to face the question of whether she should repeat her classroom lesson in discrimination. There was no question, ever, of wanting to. It was too unpleasant. But there was the more important question of whether she felt it to be a valuable exercise for the children. On balance, she had decided it was, but the presence in her classroom this year of boys and girls who were—and who knew they were—far behind other children their age in reading, called for special consideration.

It could be assumed, she felt, that any child with reading problems at the third-grade level had already tasted in his home or in school some of the bitterness of being thought inferior. A good part of her work with these children was, in fact, based on the conviction that they must lose whatever sense of inferiority they had acquired before they could be expected to profit fully from the special methods of learning to read that she used with them. To burden them with the additional weight of actually being treated as inferior, even for just a single day, raised obvious questions.

There were other factors to be considered. "One of the first things I had worried about," Jane says, "after seeing the delight with which the first year's class practiced discrimination when they were in the 'superior' group, was

whether I might be teaching the joys of discriminating along with the horrors of being discriminated against. It's a real question. I had decided, finally, that it had just not worked that
way, because for the two remaining months of
school that year, whenever we discussed it—and
the children brought it up again and again—
no child ever indicated a willingness to repeat
the exercise even for another chance at being
on top for a day. What they remembered, what
they talked about, and what they applied to
other situations, was not how good they had
felt when they were treated as superior but the
misery of being treated as inferior. That and the
pain of being separated from friends, which of
course happened on both days."

Nor was this all that gave Jane pause when
she considered whether or not to repeat the exercise. "I was far from eager to go through the
experience again myself," she says. "It ranked
high in my memory of most unpleasant chores,
and I had felt after it was finally over that first
time that I would never do it again. It's hard
work, for one thing, probably because it forces
a teacher to do deliberately what she normally
tries hardest to avoid: to deceive her students, to tell them something she knows is not
true. It's a complete reversal of ordinary good
teaching. And besides that, you work and work
to build up a good rapport with your students,
and then for two days you deliberately destroy
it, knowing you will somehow have to build it

up again when the lesson is over. That hadn't
taken long to do with the first group; inside of
half an hour, we were all good friends again.
But how could you be sure it would work that
way with a second group? And with every
child?

"Finally, there's the simple fact that it's a
sickening experience to cause children with
whom you've identified closely that much pain,
even if you're convinced that the lesson is important. I had felt like a monster picking on a
child I would normally help, singling out for
ridicule a child I would normally protect from
it. I had flinched inside myself every time I did
it. I had had to force myself to pick up the cues
the children provided me with. I had wanted
to call it off a hundred times each day. And I
had kept wanting to say to the class, 'What's
wrong with you? Why don't you stand up and
refuse to put up with this? Why don't you de-
fend each other from me?'

"Yet even as I had thought that, I had
known that I represented authority in that
room, that they had all been taught from birth
to respect authority, and that this was at least
a part of the reason they didn't resist. And isn't
that at least part of the reason that racial discrimination persists in this country? Didn't the
segregation laws in the South and don't the cus-
toms of discrimination in the North represent
the same kind of authority to adult Americans?
How many of us stand up to them? And this,

too, is a valid part of the lesson, it seems to me: that it is healthy to question authority when you know that it's wrong. Isn't that what Martin Luther King's life—and death—were all about?

"Still," Jane says with a deep sigh, "there must be a better way to teach children these lessons than the one I thought of. There must be a way to keep children from growing up into the kind of adult so many of us are, a way less drastic, less painful than this. And if we can get to the moon, we can certainly find it. There must be an expert somewhere who could tell me a better way to do this job. But so far, nobody has."

And so, in the end, Jane led her second class through the exercise that had come by now to be called "Discrimination Day." Convinced after a month with them that all of the children could handle the problems presented by it, even more convinced on the basis of the first year's results that it was an important part of the learning process, she scheduled the lesson in October, giving herself most of the school year to observe and deal with the results.

What happened during those two days was similar to what had happened the previous year, though there were some differences. One boy, for example, maintained consistently throughout the entire exercise that eye color made no difference in people. "It's not true," he said whenever Jane made a discriminatory statement. "It's not fair," he insisted whenever she gave one group an advantage over the other. When his own group was given extra recess, he still maintained that it was not right.

"You should be happy, Paul," Jane told him. "You have the right color eyes."

"But it's not true and it's not fair no matter what you say," he replied heatedly.

A second boy seemed simply to ignore the entire exercise. Without openly objecting to it, he simply proceeded to treat his friends of whatever eye color as he always had. He didn't discriminate; he wasn't depressed at being in the "inferior" group or elated at being in the "superior" group.

Because she had this class for nearly eight months after the exercise, Jane was better able to observe the long-term effects of it than she had been with the first year's group. "All through the year," she says, "they applied what they had learned to new and different situations. When the question of how we could have 'Peace on Earth' arose at Christmas time, Paul, the boy who had resisted Discrimination Day from beginning to end, said, 'We can have it by making all the grownups go through Discrimination Day.'

"Another time, when they all came in from recess, there was grumbling about the teacher who had been on playground duty. It had been going on for some time, so I asked them about it. Whether they were right or wrong I don't know, but almost all of them stoutly maintained that the teacher was always picking on the same group of boys from another third-grade classroom. 'They don't do anything wrong,' one boy said, 'but every time we go out, she just watches those same kids and bawls them out for nothing.' The others agreed. Then one child said, 'She's discriminating against them. That's what she's doing.' And suddenly everyone had the same idea: the teacher should go through Discrimination Day. Then she'd know how it feels."

When word got out that Jane had held her exercise again, a group of high school boys who rode the same school bus as several of her third-graders began taunting the youngsters. "You're the kids that have that nigger-lover for a teacher," they jeered. "You must all be nigger-lovers in that class."

"These were the older boys my third-graders had looked up to and admired and envied for three years on that same school bus," Jane says. "They were the noisy, boisterous, tough group that sat in the back of the bus each morning and afternoon, and they had always seemed quite glamorous to my young boys. But when this happened, one of my boys came strutting into the room as though he were suddenly ten feet tall. 'Boy, Mrs. Elliott,' he said, 'did I learn something on the bus this morning!' I asked him what he had learned, and he said, 'We already know more than those high school kids do. They were calling us "nigger-lovers" on the bus today. We already know that it's wrong to use the word "nigger," and we know that there's nothing wrong with being one, either. And they're in high school, and they don't even know that!'

"I was torn between guilt and pride: guilt at having exposed these nine-year-olds to such taunts and pride at their response. Because the others agreed with him."

Some weeks after the exercise, the mother of one of Jane's third-grade boys met with her at a conference. "What have you done with my son?" she asked. "He's a different boy at home. We actually look forward to his getting off the bus at night. He even treats his little brother and sister kindly. He just doesn't act like the same boy at all. What happened to him?"

"It was true," Jane says. "I had seen the same change in him at school, and it dated from Discrimination Day. From a belligerent, overbearing, unpopular boy, he had become a thoughtful, pleasant child. Almost overnight. And while he was certainly an exception in the sense of such a dramatic change, all of the children seemed to me to be more loving and much kinder to each other than before. The whole attitude in that room changed after the exercise; we were all much more comfortable with each other."

# VI

Jane Elliott's success in teaching remedial reading led, the following year, to a class of sixteen
third-graders, all of whom had difficulty with
reading. For a while, that fall of 1969, she wondered again whether she dared to introduce the
lesson in discrimination. Keeping an open mind
about it, she turned to her work with her usual
enthusiasm.

Late in the fall, with the whole class making
good progress, she decided she would give the
lesson, scheduling it mentally for about the
middle of the year. That would give her time
to establish a good relationship with each of the
children before it happened and time, afterwards, to allow the children to elaborate on
whatever they learned from it.

In a way, when the time came, it was as
though the two previous experiences had been
a sort of dress rehearsal, for meanwhile ABC

News had asked permission to send a producer and two complete camera crews to film the lesson for a network television documentary. That meant that this time whatever happened in the classroom would be ineradicably recorded on film, and an audience of millions of Americans would see it.

Arrangements for the filming were made without difficulty. Mr. Brandmill, the school principal; Donald Johnson, the superintendent; the school board; the parents of the children in the room—all gave their approval. The children, however, were told only that their class had been chosen to be filmed for television. They had no warning—and presumably no knowledge—of the Discrimination Day exercise to come.

To give the eight boys and eight girls in the class a chance to get used to the lights, cameras, microphones, and film crews—and to give the producer an opportunity to film normal school activities—it was decided to film an entire day before the exercise began. Cameras and lights were set up in the classroom on a Sunday, and when the children arrived on Monday, February 23, Room 10 had been transformed into a miniature sound stage. All equipment had been placed along one side of the room, leaving Jane and her children free to use the rest of the room as they normally would.

Jane had previously cautioned the children not to look at the cameras and to ignore the

activities of the camera crews. With few exceptions that first day, they did. She had also discussed with them the fact that the filming was
to take place during Brotherhood Week and
asked them to think about what that meant. As
it happened, two members of the eleven-man
crew were Negroes. The children seemed
scarcely to notice.

That Monday passed quickly, both for the
children and the film crews. During recess, at
the lunch hour, and before and after school, the
children chattered excitedly with the producer
and his assistant, the two cameramen and their
assistants, the three soundmen, and the electri-
cians. They watched cameras being loaded and
unloaded, looked through the lenses, tested the
microphones, and listened to their voices on the
tape recorder. A piece of film, a length of audio
tape became prizes to take home and show the
family.

When class was in session, the crews went
about their work silently and unobtrusively,
filming and recording the high points of the
day. Cameramen who had filmed everything
from riots to earthquakes, soundmen who had
recorded prize fighters and Presidents, and a
producer of documentaries on civil rights in
Mississippi and wild animals in East Africa—all
were quickly drawn into the interplay between
teacher and students, for Jane Elliott had a zest
for her work and a delight in her third-graders
that was fascinating to watch. And, of course,

the film crews, unlike the students, knew what was going to happen the following day.

The cameras were rolling when, during that day, Jane asked each child to draw a picture of her. As they bent to the task, glancing up frequently at her, a girl in the back of the room asked what color her eyes were. "Blue," Jane said, removing her glasses for a moment. "What color are yours?"

"Brown," the girl said, opening them wide.

"I wonder," Jane said casually, "how many of us have brown eyes." The drawing stopped, and the children peered at each other's eyes. When a count had been made, there were eight with blue eyes and eight with either brown or green eyes. Jane wrote the names and the eye colors on the front blackboard. Then everyone went back to his crayons. When the drawings were finished, Jane collected them. Without exception, they pictured her with a broad smile. She wondered, paging through them, how the brown-eyed children would portray her tomorrow.

Their names and eye colors were still on the blackboard when the children entered the brightly lighted room the next day. Before the bell rang, several children drifted over to where the camera crew stood quietly beside their equipment. The men were accepted now as part of the classroom, and there was little of the previous day's excitement about their presence.

54

The day began with the salute to the flag. During the singing of "God Bless America," which Jane led spiritedly from the front of the room, Raymond Hansen, a handsome boy with fair hair, bright blue eyes, and the soft, round, angelic face of a choirboy, turned almost unconsciously toward the rest of the room and, singing lustily, kept time with one hand. He was clearly a child who enjoyed school.

"Who knows a poem?" Jane asked as soon as they were seated. Hands shot up, and for the next ten minutes there were eager recitations interspersed with songs that various children suggested. Brian Saltou, a puckish boy with an infectious grin, recited "Little Orphant Annie" from beginning to end with hardly a stumble and then smiled with pleasure at his accomplishment.

Finally, Jane glanced at the calendar on the front wall and said, "This is a special week. Does anybody know what it is?"

"National Brotherhood Week," several children responded.

"What's 'brotherhood'?" Jane asked.

There was a pause and then Sandra Dohlman, a quiet child with an appealing, waifish look, asked hesitantly, "Be kind to your brothers?"

"Okay," Jane said, nodding. "Be kind to your brothers."

"Treat everyone the way you would like to be treated?" Raymond Hansen asked.

.

55

"Treat everyone the way you would like to be treated," Jane repeated. "Treat everyone as though he were your—"

"Brother," the class said in unison.

Jane took a few steps toward the door and then turned to ask, "Is there anyone in the United States that we do not treat as our brothers?"

"Yeah," several children answered.

"Who?"

Raymond Hansen answered instantly. "Black people."

"The black people," Jane said. "Who else?"

"Indians?" asked Sandra.

"Absolutely, the Indians," Jane said. "And when many people see a black person or a yellow person or a red person, what do they think? What do they sometimes say?"

Sandra made a disgusted face. "Ew, look at the dumb people," she said.

"Look at the dumb people," Jane said flatly. "What else do they think sometimes? What kinds of things do they say about black people?"

Greg Johanns, a stocky boy with an alert air, frowned and said, "They call them 'Negroos,' 'niggers,' things like that. When I used to say 'Negroes,' my father said I should call them black people. You're supposed to call them black people now."

Jane nodded and went on. "In the city and in many places in the United States, how are black people treated? How are Indians treated?

56

How are people of a different color than we are treated?"

Greg Johanns was back with an answer. "Like they're not part of this world. They don't get anything in this world."

"Why is that?" Jane asked.

"Because they're a different color," Greg replied.

When Jane asked them what they knew about black people, several children volunteered answers. "They're big," one boy answered, "the ones you see playing football on TV."

Donna Reddel, a tall girl with large brown eyes and straight brown hair, said she thought some of the black women on television were pretty, and she named a Negro singer. "I like her hair," she added.

"Some of them have hair out to here," a boy said, describing an Afro haircut with his hands.

Donna said, "Yesterday, some of the kids in the hall said, 'You have two niggers in your room.' I told my mother last night we had two black people in our room." She glanced quickly at the two Negro members of the film crew.

"Did you tell your mother anything else about them?" Jane asked.

Donna grinned. "I said I liked them."

Jane nodded. "Greg said we treat black people differently because they're a different color. Do you think that's true?"

"Sure," Raymond said.

"Do you think you know how it would feel
to be judged by the color of your skin?"

There was a thoughtful silence, and then Rex
Kozak, a short, wiry boy with blue eyes and
blond hair, nodded. "Yeah," he said doubtfully.

"Do you think you do?" Jane asked again.
Several of the children shook their heads. "Do
you think you know how it would feel to be a
black boy or girl in a school with mostly white
children?" This time there were more head-
shakers. "No," Jane said, "I don't think you
would know how that felt unless you had been
through it, would you?"

Now there was general agreement. Jane
paused. "Would you like to know?"

There was a scattering of yesses from the
class. "Well, let's see," Jane said. "Is there anything about you people that is different from
one another that we could use to make part
of you—"

"Black?" Raymond asked, before she could
finish.

Jane pursed her lips noncommittally.

"The eyes!" a girl said suddenly. "The color
of the eyes!"

"Okay," Jane agreed. "We could use the color
of your eyes. How many in here have blue
eyes?" Eight hands shot up. "Okay," Jane said,
"how many in here have brown eyes—or
green?" The hands of the other eight went up.

"It's all right there on the blackboard behind

you," a girl said, pointing, and Jane turned to look at the list.

"That's right, it is." She turned back to the class. "It might be interesting to judge people today by the color of their eyes," she said speculatively.

Three children began bouncing up and down in their seats with excitement.

"Would you like to try this?"

"Yeah!" The answer was almost a shout as the entire class was caught up in enthusiasm for the idea.

"It sounds like fun, doesn't it?" Jane asked.

"Yeah!" the whole class shouted again.

"All right. Since I'm the teacher, and I have blue eyes, I think maybe the blue-eyed people should be on top the first day."

Roy Wilson, a serious-looking boy with brown eyes, close-cropped hair, and a long, oval face, frowned with puzzlement. "You mean . . ." He stopped, unsure what she could mean.

"I mean," Jane said with finality, "the blue-eyed people are the better people in this room."

"Uh-uh!" It was Brian Saltou, his blue eyes flashing.

"Oh, yes, they are," Jane said, turning to face him. "Blue-eyed people are smarter than brown-eyed people . . ."

"Uh-uh!" Brian said again, even more forcefully. "My dad isn't stupid."

"Is your dad brown-eyed?" Jane asked.

"Yep," Brian said bluntly.

"One day you came to school and you told us that he kicked you," Jane said. There were snickers from the rest of the class.

Brian grinned and nodded, just once. "He did."

"Do you think a blue-eyed father would kick his son?" Jane asked.

"My dad would," Brian said definitely.

Jane shrugged. "My dad's blue-eyed, and he's never kicked me. Raymond's dad is blue-eyed, and he's never kicked him. Russell's dad is blue-eyed, and he's never kicked him."

Brian refused to listen. Putting his hands on his head, he jammed his arms against his ears and put his head down on his desk, ignoring her.

"What color eyes did George Washington have?" Jane asked.

Sandra Dohlman and Julie Smith, both brown-eyed, seated alongside each other, turned at this to stare at each other's eyes. "Blue?" Sandra asked, blinking, clearly hoping she was wrong.

Brian's head was up again. "Blue," he said disgustedly, "or else brown."

"Blue," Jane said. "Blue." She paused. "This is a fact. Blue-eyed people are better than brown-eyed people."

Brian shook his head vigorously.

"Are you blue-eyed or brown-eyed?" she asked him.

60

"Blue."

"Then why are you shaking your head?"

He shrugged his shoulders. "I don't know."

"Are you sure that you're right?"

He nodded once with complete assurance.

"Why? What makes you so sure that you're right?"

"I don't know," he said, and without saying it, his expression added: *but I am.*

Jane turned back to the rest of the class, and the children, who had followed the argument closely, twisted back in their seats to face the front of the room again. "Today," Jane said, when it was evident that no one else was going to contest her statements, "the blue-eyed people get five extra minutes of recess, while the brown-eyed people have to stay in."

There was a gasp of delight from the blue-eyed children, a low moan from the brown-eyed.

"The brown-eyed people do not get to use the drinking fountain," she continued. "You'll have to use the paper cups."

"Why?" asked Donna Reddel, her brown eyes wide with annoyance.

Jane repeated the question to the class. "Why?"

Greg Johanns had the answer. "Because we might catch something from them?"

Jane looked at him and nodded shortly. "We might catch something from you." She paused to let it sink in. "You brown-eyed people are not to play with the blue-eyed people on the playground, because you are not as good as blue-eyed people. You cannot play with them unless you are specifically invited to."

A number of the brown-eyed girls looked plaintively at their blue-eyed friends. "And I would suggest," Jane added, "that you blue-eyed people think twice about it before you invite a brown-eyed person to play with you today. You may not mind playing with a brown-eyed person, and you may if you wish, but you'll probably want to think about what your blue-eyed friends will think of you."

In the hush that followed, Jane moved to her desk at the back of the room. "The brown-eyed people in this room today are going to wear collars so that we can tell from a distance what color your eyes are." She picked up eight blue felt collars and a box of pins from the desk. "We aren't always close enough to see your eyes, and we want to be able to tell even when your back is turned," she said, walking back to the front of the room. "We wouldn't want to make a mistake. Now the blue-eyed people, each of you can pick out someone on whom to put a collar. So blue-eyed people each come up and get a collar."

"I will!" cried Sheila Schaefer, the only one of an inseparable threesome of girls to have blue eyes. She hesitated only a moment between her two best friends, dark-haired Susan

Ginder and slim, freckled, red-haired Julie Smith. Then she pinned the collar on Julie.

The other blue-eyed children busied themselves pinning collars on their brown-eyed classmates, but Brian Saltou remained in his seat. When Jane held out the last remaining collar, he got up reluctantly and took it, pinning it on the only brown-eyed child left without one. Then he took his seat again.

# VII

After the blue-eyed children had been given seats in the front of the room and the job of row leader in each row had been reassigned to a blue-eyed student, Jane told them to get out their English workbooks. "Turn to page 127," she said, writing the number on the blackboard.

"Is everyone ready?" she asked finally, glancing around the room. "Everyone but Laurie," she said, watching brown-eyed little Laurie Mayer squirm as she paged rapidly through her workbook. "Ready, Laurie?" she asked when Laurie had found the page. Laurie nodded, looking up unhappily through her harlequin glasses.

"She's a brown-eye!" someone jeered.

"She's a brown-eye," Jane confirmed. "You'll begin to notice today that we spend a great deal of time waiting for brown-eyed people."

65

Laurie pursed her lips unhappily, and Donna, sitting near her, flashed a brown-eyed, resentful look at Jane.

That was the way it went all morning. Whenever a brown-eyed child was slow, whenever one made a mistake, Jane made a point of picking it up. Blue-eyed children could seemingly do no wrong. As the brown-eyed children became tense and unhappy, the blue-eyed children relaxed and all but blossomed under the approving eye of their teacher. All but Brian Saltou. Brian, who had objected so strenuously at the outset to Jane's insistence that blue eyes made you better, still seemed part of neither group. He neither taunted the brown-eyed nor identified with the blue-eyed. Jane had always seen him as a kind of loner. He remained one.

At morning recess, the blue-eyed children were excused five minutes early, and they left the room in a bustle of enthusiasm. Brian went along without a visible sign of special pleasure. The brown-eyed children remained behind, working gloomily at their desks. When it was time for them to go out, they pinned their collars to their coats and trudged morosely out to the snowy playground, sullen, disgruntled, angry children. Three brown-eyed girls marched fiercely across the playground, avoiding the crowded swings, slides, and jungle gym, giving a wide berth to clusters of playing children. Their heads together, they talked furiously as they stomped briskly the length of the frozen yard.

Two brown-eyed boys slipped around a corner of the building and seated themselves, alone, on a step against the brick wall. By the time recess was over, all of the brown-eyed children had found each other and were huddled in little groups along that wall. Two girls consoled a third, who was close to tears.

It was after recess when Russell Ring, a large, good-natured, blue-eyed boy, explaining how he had got so wet, said that he had been wrestling. "You like to wrestle, don't you?" Jane asked, smiling.

"Sure," Russell said.

"He's strong, too," Rex Kozak said, laughing.

"Well, of course he's strong," Jane said. "He's got blue eyes. You must be strong, too, Rex."

"Sure," Rex said, "but not as strong as Russell."

Blue-eyed Greg Johanns, sitting next to Rex, said, "I like to fight, too. You should see what I can do to my little sister."

Jane laughed out loud. "Greg, you're always fighting with your little sister, aren't you?"

Greg smiled and nodded. "Sure. It's fun."

Later that morning, Jane, sitting with a blue-eyed reading group at a round table in the back of the room while the other children worked at their desks, reached behind her to the chalk tray for a yardstick to use as a pointer. It wasn't there. "The yardstick's gone," she said, looking quickly around the room. "I don't see the yardstick, do you?" she asked the children in the group. When one of them found it and brought it to her, she took it and stood up at the blackboard.

"Hey, Mrs. Elliott!" Raymond Hansen said excitedly. "You better keep that on your desk so if the brown people—the brown-eyed people —get out of hand . . ." His voice trailed off.

"Oh," Jane said, unable to keep a note of disapproval out of her voice, "you think if the brown-eyed people get out of hand, that would be the thing to use?"

A number of brown-eyed children had turned around to look resentfully at Raymond. Raymond backed down. "Well, no," he said.

At lunchtime, Jane stood in front of the class. "Who goes first to lunch?" she asked.

"The blue-eyes," said those with blue eyes.

"The blue-eyed people," Jane agreed. "No brown-eyed people may go back for seconds. Blue-eyed people may go back for seconds. Brown-eyed people do not."

"Why not the brown-eyes?" Brian asked with more than a trace of annoyance in his voice.

"Don't you know?" Jane asked him.

"They're not smart," Greg Johanns informed him.

"Is that the only reason?" Jane asked the class.

"You're afraid they'll take too much," Sheila Schaefer said gleefully.

"They might take too much," Jane said, nodding. "Now let's get in line, the blue-eyed people first."

As the children moved to form a double line at the door, Raymond spoke up. "You should tell the person that you go back to for dessert to watch for these collars."

Once again, Jane had difficulty concealing her annoyance at Raymond's delight in discriminating against his brown-eyed classmates. "Oh," she said finally, "you think I should alert the lunchroom help to know that these people should be treated differently?"

"The woman that you go back to for seconds!" Greg shouted. "Tell her! Tell her!"

Sheila Schaefer, securely in the front of the line with the other blue-eyed children, jumped up and down excitedly. "Yeah!" she squealed. "Yeah!"

"Probably we should do that, shouldn't we?" Jane asked.

There was a chorus of yesses from the front of the line.

During the afternoon recess, there was a brief scuffle between big, jolly, blue-eyed Russell Ring and John Benttine, smaller, quieter, and brown-eyed. John's anger at what had been happening had been smoldering inside him for hours. Even though he and Russell were close friends, he was clearly unwilling to be taunted by him.

Jane, having heard about the fight, brought it up as soon as recess was over. "What happened at recess?" she asked. "Were two of you boys fighting?"

"Russell and John were," several children reported at once.

"What happened, John?" Jane asked.

His chin all but buried in the collar around his neck, John looked up resentfully. "Russell called me names, and I hit him. Hit him in the gut."

"What did he call you?"

John's lips quivered as he answered. "Brown-eyes."

"Did you call him 'brown-eyes'?" Jane asked Russell.

Russell looked up sheepishly at her through his glasses.

"They always call us that," Roy Wilson complained from across the room.

"'Come here, brown-eyes,' that's what they say," Verla Buls said, imitating the jeering catcall.

"They were calling us 'blue-eyes'," Rex Kozak said.

"I wasn't," Susan Ginder said.

"Me and Sandy and Donna were," Roy Wilson admitted.

"Yeah," Rex agreed.

"What's wrong with being called 'brown-eyes'?" Jane asked the class.

"It means that we're stupider and—well, not that exactly," Roy Wilson said.

Before he could continue, Raymond, blue eyes bright with excitement, interrupted. "Oh, that's just the same as other people calling black people 'niggers'!"

Turning back to John, Jane asked him, "Is that the reason you hit him?" John stared at her, his brown eyes smoldering. He nodded shortly.

"Did it help?"

John shook his head.

"Did it stop him?"

He shook his head again.

"Did it make you feel better inside?"

Once more he shook his head, this time reluctantly.

Turning to Russell Ring, Jane asked, "Did it make you feel better to call him 'brown-eyes'?" Russell looked embarrassed, but he didn't answer. "Why do you suppose you called him 'brown-eyes'?"

Now Brian entered the discussion. "Why, because he has brown eyes," he said, as though anybody could see that.

"Is that the only reason?" Jane asked. "He didn't call him 'brown-eyes' yesterday, and he had brown eyes yesterday, didn't he?"

"But we just started this," a brown-eyed girl objected.

"Yeah," Brian said accusingly. "Ever since you put those blue things on them," circling his neck with a finger to indicate the blue collars the brown-eyed children wore.

The final blow for the brown-eyed children that day came when Jane sent their blue-eyed classmates off to gym without them. When the others had left the room, she faced eight scowling children. "Let's all come down here to the front of the room," she said, perching on a stool between the desks and the blackboard. They came, reluctantly, and sat on the front desks or on the floor.

"How do you feel about today?" Jane asked them.

"Awful," Donna Reddel said.

"Terrible," said red-haired Julie Smith.

"It hasn't been a very pleasant day, has it?" Jane asked. They agreed that it hadn't. "Why?"

"Because we've got brown eyes," Roy said.

"Have you learned anything today that you didn't know before?"

For a moment there was only a glum silence. Then Sandra Dohlman spoke. "It's better to have blue eyes," she said miserably.

"Can you do anything about the color of your eyes?"

Sandra shook her head.

"You can't change them, can you?"

They all shook their heads.

"Do you wish you had blue eyes?"

"Yes," several of them answered.

"Why?"

"Well, because you get to go to recess early," Susan Ginder said.

"And you get seconds at lunch," Laurie Mayer said.

"And you get to go to gym," Julie Smith added.

"And why is that?" Jane asked.

"Because you have blue eyes," a number of them responded.

"And that's the only reason?"

"Blue eyes are better," Sandra said. "They get everything."

"And we have to wear these stupid collars," Donna said angrily.

"If you took the collars off, would that change anything?" Jane asked.

"No," several of the children said.

"Why not?"

"Well, we'd still have brown eyes," Susan Ginder said.

"That's right," Jane said. "Brown eyes are the problem, aren't they?"

A number of them nodded morosely.

"You remember when we started this, we said we'd like to find out how it feels to be discriminated against. Do you think you know now how it feels?"

"We sure do," Roy said.

"How does it feel?"

"It feels awful."

"You feel like you can't do anything," Julie Smith said.

"I feel mean," Donna said.

"It's like you don't have any friends anymore," Verla Buls said, picking at her collar.

"Would you like to take these collars off?" Jane asked.

"Yeah," they all said dubiously, not quite daring to hope.

"Take them off." The collars were off in no time. Jane collected them. "I lied to you today," she said. "It wasn't true when I said that blue-eyed people are better than brown-eyed people. That's not true at all. Brown-eyed people are every bit as good as blue-eyed people."

"Yeah," Roy said, brightening.

"They are," Jane said. "And tomorrow, the blue-eyed people are going to find out how it feels to be discriminated against for the color of their eyes."

"You mean they're going to have to wear those stupid collars?" Donna asked, still suspicious.

Jane nodded, and Donna's face was transformed by a wide grin. "And you're going to have five extra minutes of recess while they stay in," Jane added.

Donna licked her lips in anticipation. "Oh, boy!"

"Boy, are we going to show them!" Roy exclaimed, throwing his arm over John's shoulder. John, who had said little since the fight at recess, smiled slightly, and then withdrew into himself again. The other children wriggled with excitement.

"Are you looking forward to tomorrow?" Jane asked.

"Yeah!" they answered.

"Are you going to treat them the way they treated you today?"

"Yeah!"

"How did they treat you today?"

"Awful," several of them said.

"And that's how you're going to treat them tomorrow?"

This time the response was less enthusiastic.

"Do you remember how you felt today?"

They nodded.

"And that's the way you want them to feel tomorrow?"

"Well, it's only fair," Donna protested. "They were mean to us today. Now it's our turn."

"That's right," Sandra said. "They did it first."

"So tomorrow you're going to give it right back to them, is that it?"

"Well, why not?" Donna asked.

Julie Smith shrugged her shoulders. "Maybe not as bad as they did," she said.

"But you do want them to know how it feels, is that right?"

The dilemma was clear on most of their faces. They wanted to get even, to have their revenge, but they knew there was something wrong in it.

75

"Well, but can't we at least have extra recess and all that?" Laurie Mayer asked plaintively. "They got that."

"Oh, you're going to have all the privileges they had today," Jane said. "I'm just wondering how you're going to treat them. They treated you badly, and I wonder if you're going to treat them badly, too."

Susan Ginder, who with Julie Smith had lost the company of their best friend, blue-eyed Sheila Schaefer, that day, had not failed to note Sheila's delight in discriminating against both of them. She was intent on fighting back. John Benttine, who had fought over being called "brown-eyes," was clearly so glad this day was over that he had little room in his thoughts for the next one. Perhaps, by defending himself, he also felt that he had had his revenge.

"How many of you think you're going to give the blue-eyed people a bad time tomorrow?" Jane asked. Most of the hands went up, though there was something tentative about some of them. "Well," Jane said, "it will be interesting to see what happens tomorrow."

"They won't like it," Verla Buls said thoughtfully.

"No, I'm sure they won't," Jane agreed. Then, glancing at the clock, seeing there was still time before the others returned from gym, she asked, "Did you believe me when I told you that blue-eyed people were better than brown-eyed people?"

76

Four or five of them said yes. Others shrugged.

"Did you think it might be true?"

Now nearly all of them nodded.

"Why?"

"Well," Roy said slowly. "You told us."

"But why did you believe me?"

There was silence.

"Would you have believed me if I'd told you the moon was made of green cheese?"

"No," they said, shaking their heads.

"Then why did you believe this?"

Donna said, "I didn't know whether to believe you or not at first, but then, later, it seemed like it was true."

"Why?"

"Well," Sandra said, "because we just couldn't do anything right today."

"Oh," Jane said. "So when I told you you weren't as good as they were, you didn't feel as good anymore. Is that it?"

Roy nodded. "I just couldn't think straight today."

"Why?" Jane asked. "Because you have brown eyes?"

"No," Roy said with finality.

"Then why?"

"Well, because we had to wear those collars and . . ."

"Because you were picking on us all day," Donna said flatly. "That's why. I told Verla I was going to tell my mother tonight that you'd been mean to us all day. I wasn't going to come to school tomorrow."

"Neither was I," Verla said.

"Do you think now you'll come to school?" Jane asked with a smile.

"I sure will!" Donna said, smiling broadly. Everybody laughed.

Before the others returned to the classroom to be dismissed for the day, Jane cautioned the brown-eyed children on the need for secrecy about what she had told them. "We don't want them to know until tomorrow what's going to happen," she said, "so you will all have to act sad when they come back and on the bus tonight and on the bus tomorrow morning. Do you think you can do that."

Eight beaming faces tried desperately to look unhappy.

"You'll have to do a lot better than that," Jane said, laughing at them.

1. Of her unique lessons in discrimination, teacher Jane Elliott (here being interviewed by ABC News Correspondent Bill Beutel) said in 1970, "I wanted my third-graders to learn about discrimination from the inside, by experiencing it. I hope when they are involved, later on, in similar situations, they will recognize what the other person must be feeling—and pull back."

2. Donna Reddel wears the collar symbolizing membership in the "inferior" brown-eyed group.

3. The happy blue-eyes go first to lunch. Front to rear: Russell Ring, Tammy Bill, Rex Kozak, Sheila Schaefer, Raymond Hansen, Greg Johanns, Brian Saltou. Unhappy brown-eyes, wearing collars and denied second servings, follow: Laurie Mayer, Verla Buls, John Benttine, Donna Reddel, Julie Smith, Susan Ginder, Sandra Dohlman (mostly hidden), Roy Wilson.

4. After a recess scuffle on the playground, John Benttine admits under questioning, "Russell called me names, and I hit him. Hit him in the gut." The name Russell called him: "Brown-eyes."

5. The next day, with the brown-eyes designated "superior," blue-eyed Tammy Bill, Greg Johanns, and Russell Ring (partly hidden) are collared by Laurie Mayer, John Benttine, and Donna Reddel. Donna chortles, "I've been waiting all day to put this on Russell."

6. Brown-eyed Susan Ginder smiles delightedly when Jane Elliott points out to a blue-eyed child who had forgotten his glasses, "Susan Ginder has brown eyes. She didn't forget her glasses."

7. Blue-eyed Raymond Hansen, an eager discriminator the first day, turns glum when the roles are reversed. On top: "I felt like a king, like I ruled them brown-eyes. Like I was better than them. Happy." On the bottom: "I felt down, unhappy, like I couldn't do anything, like I was tied up and couldn't get loose."

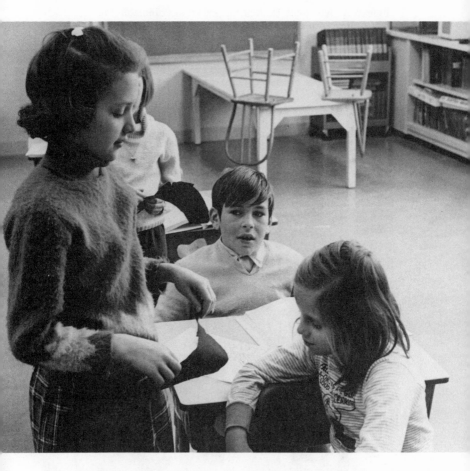

8. Alone of the children, Brian Saltou (center) resisted at every step the idea that either group was superior. Singled out for Mrs. Elliott's scorn on his "inferior" day, he waited until she looked away, then mouthed a silent message more eloquent than any curse.

9. The third-grade classroom was transformed into a miniature sound stage for the filming of the ABC News documentary, "The Eye of the Storm." Producer William Peters (reading) later wrote *A Class Divided* about Jane Elliott's lesson in discrimination. Two members of the film crew, at right, were Negroes.

10. Jane Elliott had instructed the children to ignore the activities of the camera crews. With few exceptions, they did.

11. Cameraman Vince Gaito shows the children how film is loaded in a film magazine during recess.

12. Eleven of the sixteen students in Jane Elliott's third-grade class of 1970 returned to Riceville, Iowa, for a reunion with their teacher in 1984. Pictured in the schoolyard are (from left): Donna Reddel (May), Roy Wilson, Susan Ginder (Rolland), Verla Buls, Julie Smith (Trampel), Sandra Dohlman (Burke), teacher Jane Elliott, Rex Kozak, Milton Wolthoff, Raymond Hansen, Brian Saltou, and Sheila Schaefer (Flaherty).

# VIII

They came into the classroom next morning looking much as they had the day before: the blue-eyed children cheerful, breezy, self-confident; the brown-eyed children lethargic and solemn. Only occasionally, in a glance or a nudge, as the brown-eyed children pinned their collars on again and took their seats, could their suppressed excitement be glimpsed.

When the opening exercises were over, a blue-eyed boy spoke up. "I know what's going to happen today. My brother told me you're going to turn it around."

"Oh, he did, did he?" Jane said.

"Yes. He said you're going—"

"Just a minute," Jane said, and the boy stopped. She looked away from him and at the rest of the class. Donna had a hand clasped across her mouth, hiding a grin. "Yesterday," Jane said, "I told you that brown-eyed people

79

aren't as good as blue-eyed people. That wasn't true. I lied to you yesterday."

Brian Saltou shook his head, shrugged heavily, and said, "Oh, boy, here we go again."

Jane ignored him. "The truth is that brown-eyed people are better than blue-eyed people."

A sprinkling of delighted laughter came from the brown-eyed children. The faces of the blue-eyed sobered. Jane, glancing quickly around the room, saw Russell Ring squinting up at her with his pale blue eyes.

"Russell, where are your glasses?"

"I forgot them."

"You forgot them. And what color are your eyes?"

He stared at her sheepishly and then looked around him, like a boy caught swimming naked. "Blue," he admitted finally. The brown-eyed children squealed with pleasure.

"Laurie Mayer has brown eyes, and she didn't forget her glasses. Susan Ginder has brown eyes. She didn't forget her glasses." Susan leaned out from her desk to smirk at Russell. He grinned with embarrassment and looked away. "Russell Ring has blue eyes, and what about his glasses?" Jane continued.

"He forgot them!" the brown-eyed children answered joyfully.

Brian Saltou, studiously ignoring the conversation, had taken a tiny model car from his desk and begun to play with it, studying its wheels intently. Jane saw him.

"All these brown-eyed people are listening to what we're saying," Jane continued. "Look at Brian." The children swung around in their chairs. "Are blue-eyed people good listeners?"

"No!"

Without a flicker of recognition that he was being talked about, Brian continued to study the car.

"Brian, will you put that down, please?" Jane asked.

Even now, he did not look up, but he slipped the car back into his desk.

"Thank you." Jane took a step toward Greg Johanns. "Yesterday, we were visiting, and Greg said, 'Boy, I like to hit my little sister as hard as I can. That's fun.'" Greg winced, putting one hand to his face as though recoiling from a blow. "What does that tell you about blue-eyed people?" Jane asked.

"They're naughty," a brown-eyed girl said.

"They fight a lot," said another.

"Are blue-eyed people as civilized as brown-eyed people?" Jane asked.

"No," the brown-eyed children answered.

"The brown-eyed people may take off their collars," Jane said, "and each of you may put your collar on a blue-eyed person."

Before she had finished, Donna Reddel, eyes dancing, her face beaming with pleasure, had whipped off her collar and was scurrying up the aisle to Russell Ring's desk. Pinning the collar around his neck, she looked up at Jane. "I've been waiting all day to put this on Russell," she chortled. Russell blushed helplessly.

Raymond Hansen, who the day before had been full of ideas of ways to discipline the brown-eyed children, sat glumly, the corners of his mouth pulled down, as a collar was pinned on him. Of all the brown-eyed children, John Benttine seemed the least anxious to stigmatize a blue-eyed child with a collar. He still had one in his hand when all the blue-eyed children but Brian Saltou wore them. Almost reluctantly, then, the boy who had fought being called "brown-eyes" crossed the room to the desk of the boy who had fought the entire exercise.

Brian sat motionless, totally without expression, as John pinned the collar around his neck. Then, as John left, he put his head down on the desk, elbows against his ears, in the position he had assumed the day before.

Jane ran quickly through the rules for the day. "The brown-eyed people get five extra minutes of recess," she said. "You blue-eyed people are not allowed to be on the playground equipment at any time. You blue-eyed people are not to play with the brown-eyed people unless you are invited . . ." Tammy Bill, a blue-eyed girl with short, straight hair, pouted unhappily as the list grew longer.

When they had changed the row leaders to brown-eyed children and it came time to move the brown-eyed children to the front of the room, Brian lifted his head from his desk and, without getting up, scraped his chair and desk backwards to the new position. Then he put his head down again, blocking out Jane's voice with his arms. In a moment, though, it was clear that he could still hear.

Jane said, "Brown-eyed people are better than blue-eyed people."

Brian lifted his elbows and banged them hard on his desk.

Jane said, "They are cleaner than blue-eyed people."

Brian banged his elbows again.

Jane said, "They are more civilized than blue-eyed people."

Once more, Brian punctuated her sentence with a bang.

"They are smarter than blue-eyed people, and if you don't believe it, look at Brian."

There was a rustle as all of the children turned to look. Brian's head was still down.

"Do blue-eyed people know how to sit in a chair?" Jane asked. "Very sad. Very, very sad."

Brian's head was up now, and he glared defiantly at Jane. As she looked away, his lips began to move in a silent message he dared not say aloud. His expression said it all. No curse could have been more eloquent.

That was the day that Greg Johanns got up quietly from his chair and went to the sink for a drink. Observing the printed sign that read

"Brown" on the drinking fountain, he took a paper cup from the box and filled it at the tap. After drinking, he walked to the wastebasket and threw the cup away. He was halfway back to his seat when Jane's voice stopped him.

"Greg, what did you do with that cup?"

He stared at her.

"Will you please go and get that cup and put your name on it and keep it at your desk?" As he turned to obey, she continued. "Blue-eyed people are wasteful."

That was also the day that Russell Ring, returning from morning recess, unpinned the blue collar from his coat, put the pin between his lips as he hung the coat in his locker, and, when another boy slapped him on the back, swallowed the pin. Surprised but unhurt, he hurried to Jane. "I ate a pin," he told her.

"Are you sure, Russell?" she asked worriedly.

"Yes." He explained how it had happened.

Putting the class to work, Jane took him to the nurse's office, where they called his mother. Assured that he would be taken immediately to the hospital for X-rays, she left him and returned to the class. The strain of the exercise had already taken a heavy toll of Jane's emotions. This incident was almost too much. Worried about Russell, she wondered if she could keep her mind on what she was doing. At the classroom door, she had an almost irresistible impulse to call the whole thing off. Then, knowing she could not abandon the lesson in the middle, she squared her shoulders and re-entered the room.

"Russell swallowed a pin," she told the class calmly, "and he's being taken to the hospital. They'll take X-rays to find out where the pin is. I'm sure he'll be all right, and I'll tell you as soon as we have news of him."

The children accepted her explanation quietly, and Jane quickly put them to work. John Benttine, at the blackboard to write a contraction, was given a brief lesson in making a proper W. When he had mastered it, Jane said, "Now, that's beautiful writing! Brown-eyed people learn fast, don't they? Boy, do brown-eyed people learn fast!"

And the brown-eyed people did learn fast that day. The day before, running through a pack of flash cards against a stop watch, a reading group of brown-eyed children had taken five and a half minutes to sound out the various phonic combinations on the cards. Now, the same children sped through the same card pack in less than half that time. A blue-eyed reading group had gone through the card pack in three minutes the day before. Today, wearing their blue collars, they took four minutes and eighteen seconds.

As in everything else during those two days, Jane had consciously aided the "superior" group, turning the cards faster, ignoring minor errors. With the "inferior" group, she had insisted on absolute accuracy, giving them no help at all. Still, even allowing for the difference her own deliberate bias had made, she was convinced that there had been a real difference between the speed of each group on the two days. "If nothing else," she says, "both groups went through the pack much faster on the days they were supposedly 'superior' than they ever had before. And in everything else they did on those two days, it was clear that the children that had been labeled inferior were, in fact, behaving as though they were inferior, while the 'superior' children performed in a consistently superior manner."

After the brown-eyed children had sped through the phonic card pack that second day, Jane congratulated them. "You went faster than I ever had anyone go through the card pack," she said, smiling at their excitement and pleasure. "Why couldn't you get them yesterday?"

"We had those collars on," Donna Reddel said. The others agreed.

"Oh," Jane said. "You think the collars kept you—"

"We couldn't think with those collars on," Roy Wilson said excitedly. "My eyes just kept going around and around."

"Oh," Jane said again, "and you couldn't think as well with the collars on."

When the blue-eyed children, who had done so well the day before, did poorly on the card pack, Raymond spoke up. "I knew we weren't going to make it."

"What happened?" Jane asked.

"We went down," Rex Kozak said.

"Why? What were you thinking of?"

"This," said Rex, lifting his collar.

"Why?" Jane asked.

"It itches my neck."

"Oh," Jane said. "Do you think if we took it off, you'd do better?"

Rex looked at her and then shook his head. "No."

"Then it isn't the collar?"

"No."

"What is it?"

"Blue eyes," Raymond said.

"Well, we could take the collars off," Jane said, "but we can't change the color of our eyes, can we?"

"No," Raymond said glumly.

"I hate today," Jane said suddenly.

"You do? I hate it, too," Rex said with enthusiasm.

"Because I'm blue-eyed," Jane added.

"See, I am, too," Rex explained.

"It's not funny; it's not fun; it's not pleasant," Jane said emphatically. "This is a filthy, nasty word called 'discrimination.' We're treating people in a certain way because they are different from the rest of us. Is that fair?"

"No," they answered in unison.

"Nothing fair about it. We didn't say this was going to be a fair day, did we?"

"No."

"And it isn't. It's a horrid day."

Still, it was not as horrid as the day before. The brown-eyed children, perhaps because they remembered how it had felt, did not discriminate against their blue-eyed classmates with quite the same zeal as the latter had against them the previous day. There were no fights. Yet the blue-eyed children, having been treated as superior the previous day, reacted to their sudden fall from grace with the same depression, the same tension, the same anger as had their brown-eyed classmates. Raymond Hansen later put it succinctly. Of the first day, he said, "I felt like a king, like I ruled them brown-eyes. Like I was better than them. Happy." The second day, he said, "I felt down, unhappy, like I couldn't do anything, like I was tied up and couldn't get loose."

On both days of the exercise, Jane had the children draw pictures of her. Without exception, the "superior" group saw her as happy and smiling, while the "inferior" group portrayed her as a frowning scold. In pictures the children drew of themselves each day, the differences in the way they felt were dramatized even more strongly. Roy Wilson's drawing of himself on his "inferior" day was half the size

88

of his drawing on his "superior" day. Hairless, mouth turned down, his clothes lacking completely in detail, his first day's image of himself was eloquent testimony to his confused sense of depression. In contrast, on the second day, the large, well-drawn figure sported a happy smile, a checked shirt, a turned-up nose, and short, blond hair.

Eyelashes and eyebrows appeared along with a happy smile in Donna's picture of herself on the day she was treated as superior. They had been missing from the previous day's drawing. Laurie Mayer saw herself with tears streaming from her brown eyes, her hands in tight fists on her "inferior" day.

Milton Wolthoff, a quiet, blue-eyed boy who had done little to call attention to himself on either day, drew the most spectacularly different pictures of himself. On his "superior" day, his image all but filled the bright yellow page, and above his happy, smiling face, an angelic figure, also smiling, danced on his head waving a sign reading, "Happy Days." Colored balloons and streamers surrounded the angel. On his "inferior" day, Milton appeared at the very bottom of a solid black page, a tiny miserable figure with a devil, complete with horns and pitchfork, atop his head.

John Benttine, the boy who had hit Russell Ring on his day on the bottom, drew himself tied by his blue collar to a post, holding in his hand a sign obviously addressed to Jane. "You crab," it read. The sign in his hand the next day read simply, "Happy." Raymond Hansen drew himself as pink and smiling the day he had felt like a king. On the other day, he drew himself as a Negro.

Toward the end of that second day, Jane was called to the office. When she returned to the classroom, she told the children that Russell was in the hospital, that they had located the pin, that he was all right, but that he would stay in the hospital for a day or so. Then she asked them to come down to the front of the room. They gathered around the low stool on which she sat, seating themselves on the floor or on the front desks.

"What did you people who are wearing blue collars find out today?" she asked when all was quiet.

"I know what they felt like yesterday," Raymond said.

"I do, too," Greg said emphatically.

"How did they feel yesterday?" Jane asked.

"Like a dog on a leash," Greg said.

"Like you're chained up in a prison and they threw the key away," Raymond said.

"Should the color of some other person's eyes have anything to do with how you treat them?" Jane asked.

There was a unanimous "No."

"All right, then should the color of their skin?"

This time the "No" was louder.

"Should you judge people by the color of their skin?"

"No."

"You're going to say that today," Jane said, "and this week, and probably all the time you're in this room. You'll say, 'No-o-o, Missus Elliott,'" she chanted in a mocking, singsong way. "Every time I ask that question. Then, when you see a black man or an Indian or someone different from you walking down the street, are you going to say, 'Ha, ha, look at that silly-looking thing?'"

Their answer was almost indignant. "No!" they shouted, and then Raymond and Donna together picked up Jane's previous intonation and, the others joining in, they all said, "No-o-o, Missus Elliott," with sarcastic sweetness.

Jane laughed and then turned serious again. "Does it make any difference whether their skin is black or white?"

"No."

"Or yellow? Or red?"

"No."

"Is that how you decide whether people are good or bad?"

"No."

"Is that what *makes* people good or bad?"

"No."

"Let's take these collars off."

Greg, fumbling for the pin, said, "I'd like to just jerk it off if I could."

In a minute, the collars were off—all except Brian Saltou's. Brian sat on a desk ignoring the others as they began handing their collars to Jane.

"What would you like to do with them?" Jane asked.

"Burn them!" Raymond said.

"Throw them away!" Greg shouted.

"Go ahead!" Jane shouted back at him.

There was a rush for the wastebasket and through the noise of excited chatter a boy's voice could be heard advising, "Don't eat the pin like Russell did!" Jane winced.

When all the other blue-eyed children had thrown away their collars, Brian still sat on the desk top wearing his. "Aren't you going to take your collar off, Brian?" Jane asked.

He shook his head.

"Why not?"

"I like it," he said, smiling slightly.

"You like it," Jane repeated. Brian nodded. "Everyone else has taken his collar off, but you're going to keep yours on." He nodded again. "Why?"

"I just like it, that's all," he said.

"All right," Jane said. "Keep it on."

Instantly, his hands went to the collar. He took it off, folding it neatly.

"Don't you want to throw it away?" Jane asked him.

"No."

"Why not?"

"I'm going to keep it. I'm going to take it home."

"And what do you plan to do with it at home?"

"I'm going to put it on my dog."

"You're going to put it on your dog?"

"Yeah," Brian said. "I'll put it on him for a tail. He just has a little-bitty screw tail."

Jane paused for a moment. "I think you'd better throw the collar away, Brian," she said firmly. "All the others have, and I think you'd better, too."

Brian looked at her as though to decide if he could defy her any longer. Then he slid off the desk and went to the wastebasket, and while the other children, rejoicing in their reunion, struggled to get nearer to each other, the boys with their arms around each other, the girls hugging each other in relief, Brian fiercely tore, bit, and ripped the collar until it was in shreds. Finally, he returned to the group, but ignoring the fact that all were now on the floor, he perched himself again on the desk, with them but not a part of them.

"Now you know a little bit more than you knew at the beginning of the week," Jane was saying.

"Yes," they answered.

"A lot more," Raymond added.

"Do you know a little bit more than you wanted to?"

Their exuberance ran over, and in a single,

jeering voice, they chanted, "Ye-e-es, Missus Elliott!"

"This isn't an easy way to learn it, is it?"

Once again, they chanted, "No-o-o, Missus Elliott!"

Jane, pretending anger, shouted at them, "Oh, will you stop that!"

They broke up with laughter, the boys rolling backwards away from her, the girls clutching each other, tears in their eyes. It took a few minutes before they had begun to settle down again.

"Okay," Jane said, "now let's all sit down here together, blue eyes and brown eyes. Does it make any difference what color your eyes are?"

"No!" they shouted, beginning to laugh again.

"Okay," she said, smiling at them, "now are you back together again?"

"Yes!" they shouted, and the boys, arms around each other, began swaying back and forth like a row of students in the cheering section of a football stadium.

"Does that feel better?"

"Yes!"

Sheila, Susan, and Julie, the three inseparables, sat close to each other, Sheila in the middle, with tears of relief and joy streaming down her face; the others comforting her. "What's the matter, Sheila?" Jane asked, and Sheila laughed and cried and wiped at her eyes.

"She's crying," Julie said, on the verge of tears herself.

"Feel better now?" Jane asked, and Sheila managed to nod. "Miserable situation, isn't it?" Jane asked. Sheila sniffed and nodded again, and the other girls hugged her.

"Does that feel like being home again, girls?" Jane asked, smiling at them.

This time they all three nodded, sniffing.

"Okay," Jane said, "who knows a song?"

"'Paw-Paw Patch'!" someone shouted.

"All right," Jane said, and then singing, "'Where, O where is sweet little Sheila?'" started them all laughing again.

"'Where, O where is sweet little Sheila? Where, O where is sweet little Sheila?'" they sang, laughing and pointing at Sheila, who laughed and cried and wiped at her eyes.

"'Way down yonder in the paw-paw patch!'" they shouted.

"Let's do it!" Jane cried, standing up. "Everybody get a partner!"

They scrambled to their feet, milling around, choosing partners.

"Do we have to have girls for partners, Mrs. Elliott?" Roy asked pleadingly.

Jane laughed out loud. "No, Roy, you don't have to have girls."

The boys cheered lustily and paired off. The girls hugged each other, jumping up and down. Quickly a double row was formed, but with Russell Ring gone, they were one boy short. The extra boy, of course, was Brian.

"Come on, Brian," Jane said, still laughing.

"I'm sorry, but it looks like you're stuck with me." Brian grimaced, grinned, and took her hand. They were still singing and dancing when the bell rang.

# IX

In the weeks immediately following those two
days in February, 1970, Jane Elliott was struck
by the undeniable improvement in the work of
her students. "Four of them in particular," she
says, "Rex Kozak, Sheila Schaefer, Julie Smith,
and Greg Johanns, simply flew. It was like nothing I've ever seen. They just caught fire. When
the class took Stanford Achievement Tests in
April, I simply couldn't wait for the machine-
scored results; I corrected the tests myself to
see if what I had observed was true. It was.
Rex Kozak, for example, had gained two years
in reading ability and four and five years in
everything else. In just a single year."

Sheila Schaefer had also gained two full
years in reading ability. Walking to recess with
her one day, Jane told her how well she was
doing. "Your grades have done nothing but go

up, up, up, ever since Discrimination Day," she said. "What happened to you?"

Sheila smiled happily. "I found out I was just as good as you said I was. You told me I could do anything, and I can. *I'm smart!*"

Jane is somewhat at a loss to explain the relevance of Discrimination Day to learning, because, as she puts it, "I had been telling Sheila and all the other children how capable they were since the beginning of the school year. Yet it wasn't until after the exercise that they really began to soar. I suppose the sharp contrast between the kind of work they did on one day and the next might have something to do with it, but I really don't know. I wish someone could tell me how to get these results without putting children through such torture."

As in previous years, Jane's students continued to bring up the lessons they had learned through the exercise, to apply them to other situations, and to exhibit a sharp interest in anything that smacked even remotely of discrimination. "I think," Jane says, "if it has done nothing else for the children who have been through it, the exercise has widened their worlds. It has made them look beyond themselves. It has helped them relate to other people. I think, too, it has helped teach them not to take at face value everything everybody says. It's made them think about things in a way they haven't before, with a kind of healthy skepticism. And I think it makes children feel differently about themselves. It must, because their performance changes, academically and socially."

Once the exercise had begun, the children, caught up in the intense, conflicting emotions of the new and absorbing experience, had all but ignored the presence of the television film crews. Once it was over, they awaited the broadcast of the documentary with unconcealed impatience. It came, finally, on May 11, broadcast over the ABC Television Network under the title "The Eye of the Storm." Most of Riceville watched it.

Some Riceville adults were put off by a bit of narration in the first few minutes of the program, a line that described the community as "relatively poor." But the children in Jane's class were all but mesmerized at seeing themselves on television. Writing about it the next day in class, most told how moved their parents and relatives had been. "My mother almost cried" was a much-repeated line. Some of the children were surprised at how they had looked. "I didn't know how unhappy I was the second day," Raymond Hansen wrote. For all, living through the experience a second time had called up many of the emotions they had experienced on those two days three months earlier.

Brian Saltou, who had held out against Jane's discriminatory statements and actions, was, of course, a sort of star of the program. For weeks afterwards, he walked tall and proud. Rex Kozak told the class of being called a "movie star" by children on the school bus. Jane asked him if he minded. "It was fun," he said, grinning broadly.

A deluge of letters descended on the school after the broadcast, and the class put up a map of the United States and stuck pins in it to indicate the source of each of them. By the end of the school year, forty-four states were represented. "I read most of the letters to the class," Jane says, "all but the worst of the racist ones. More than ninety-five percent of the mail was favorable, but I felt the children should know that not everyone agreed with what we had done or even what they had learned.

"The morning after the broadcast, in fact, a man had called the school from somewhere in the South and left a message for me: 'I saw your phony sideshow on TV last night. Garbage, garbage, garbage. Fake, fake, fake.'

"I told the children, and we discussed what he might have meant. In the end, we concluded that he must have thought the exercise had been made up, that the children were simply acting out roles that had been assigned to them, knowing all the time it was a sort of game; that the whole thing had been, in effect, a play presented as reality. It was obvious, of course, that he didn't approve of the lesson. But this idea that the children were pretending to feel what they expressed, that they were acting, either for me or for the television cameras; that they could not actually have believed themselves to be inferior or superior so quickly after having been told it was a classroom exercise—this sense of disbelief was present in many of the letters we received. Reading them, I remembered how difficult it had been for me to accept it when I myself had seen it happen the first time.

"I have no final explanation for it—this absolutely real acceptance of the roles assigned them. And I don't blame other people for finding it hard to believe. But it has happened just that way each time I have done it. If it proves anything, I suppose it proves how susceptible human beings—and particularly children—are to a voice of authority.

"But even more pernicious, it also illustrates how the results of discrimination tend to create and confirm prejudice. It's a simple enough equation: choose a group, discriminate against it, force it by your discrimination to look and act inferior, and then point to the way it looks and acts as proof of its inferiority. A man who has been forced to bow and scrape will look to the outsider like a man who wants to bow and scrape. Eventually, he may even look that way to himself. A child who has been denied a decent education will become an uneducated adult. To those who didn't see—or refuse to recognize—the denial, he will seem simply stupid.

"I have asked each class that has gone through this exercise why they believed me when I said that one group or the other was inferior. The answer has always been the same. They believed me at first, tentatively, because I said it was so, because I was the teacher. Later, they believed me because they *saw* it was so. And, of course, they *had* seen it. Didn't the 'inferior' group do inferior work? Weren't they constantly having to be corrected? Didn't they become sulky, inattentive, and unhappy? And isn't that precisely what we all do when we discriminate against Negroes in employment and then castigate them as unable to do anything but sweep floors?"

To the racist letters that Jane received and read to her class, the children's reaction was healthy and intelligent. "They decided, reluctantly, I think, that there were adults who simply didn't know what they now knew," Jane says. "It gave them an even greater sense of the importance of the lesson, I suspect. And I hope it reinforced their determination to think for themselves."

As for Jane Elliott, her life, too, has been changed somewhat by the broadcasting of her lesson in discrimination. In succeeding months, she appeared on a number of television programs, explaining again what she had done and why. She addressed several professional and educational groups at their request. In the fall of 1970, she was chosen to be a member of a panel of the White House Conference on

Children and Youth. Word of her classroom exercise has spread far from the classroom.

In Riceville itself, the reaction both to the television program and to Jane's exercise has been overwhelmingly favorable. There have been some critics. Some, motivated by a frank antagonism to Negroes, have complained privately that she should not be teaching school children that Negroes are the equal of whites. Others, annoyed perhaps by the sudden notoriety of someone who grew up in their own small town, have grumbled that she is getting too big for her boots. Such responses could have been anticipated.

But there has been little but praise of the exercise from educators and psychologists. In this category, Jane is surely her own severest critic. "I've wondered, each time I've done it, if what I'm doing is right," she says. "I've worried, each time, about the possibility of hurting a child. And I've wished, each time, that someone would show me another way, a better way, a less painful way to teach children that discrimination is wrong. What I hope, of course, is that these children will retain at least something of what they've learned in these lessons, that when they become involved, later on, in situations that feel similar to the one they experienced here, they will recognize, consciously or unconsciously, what the other person must be feeling, and pull back.

"But more than that, I hope they will retain

the knowledge gained in this painful way that discrimination based on race or color or religion or any other arbitrary difference between people is illogical and irrational, that it makes no sense, and even worse, that unless they think hard about it, it can be imposed on them from the outside. I hope they know now and for all time that just because someone says something is true, just because society acts as though a fact were established, doesn't make it so. I want them to think, to reason, to question. I hope I've given them at least a starting tool to work in that direction.

"I'm not so naïve that I think this single exercise is going to change the world—or even Riceville," Jane says. "But we have to start somewhere if we hope to live in a society free of the irrationality of racism. I'm a teacher. I work with children. This is simply where I started."

# X

*That is how the book ended when it was first published in 1971. What follows is new. In part, it is an attempt to answer some of the questions raised, or at least left unanswered, in the original edition. Primarily though, it is simply a continuation of the story of that third-grade class divided by eye color in 1970 and of the teacher who divided it. As the producer–director–writer of "The Eye of the Storm" and the author of* A Class Divided, *I have necessarily become a character in this continuation.*

W. P.

The broadcast of "The Eye of the Storm" in May 1970 brought the first news of Jane Elliott's lesson in discrimination to millions of Americans. Television critics gave high praise to both Jane and the film, and ABC News repeated the documentary three times in the space of a year. Later, the program received numerous awards, including the prestigious George Foster Peabody Award.

Beginning with its first broadcast, the documentary seemed to take on a life of its own. The demand for prints (and later video cassettes) of the film was almost immediate, and before long it was being used as an educational tool by every branch of the armed forces, the National Security Agency, the State Department, and dozens of other federal, state, and local government agencies; by corporations, labor unions, and churches; by high school and college educators, civic groups, and human relations organizations. It quickly became (and for the next sixteen years would remain) one of the best-selling television films in educational distribution.

Shortly after the initial broadcast, a publisher asked me to write a book about Jane Elliott and her exercise, and the first edition of *A Class Divided*, published in 1971, was the result. Before the book came out, *Reader's Digest* published a condensation as its lead article. A year later, the book was brought out in paperback. It was clear that Jane Elliott's lesson in discrimination had struck a sensitive chord in the nation's psyche.

While more and more Americans were learning about her and her lesson and increasing numbers of organizations were using the film as a teaching tool, Jane continued to teach the lesson to her own students. Over the years since 1970, she has used the exercise with a

fourth third-grade class and—after transferring
to Riceville's junior high school—with four different groups of seventh- and eighth-graders.
Each time, the immediate results were similar
to those she had observed with her previous
classes. And while there was still no way for
her to know how deep or enduring an impression the lesson was making on her students,
there were indications that it was having at
least some lasting effects.

One such sign came when a University of
Northern Iowa scholar compared the racial attitudes of Riceville students in the third
through sixth grades with those of a similar
Iowa community nearby. He found the Riceville students less racist. A comparison of the
Riceville students who had taken Jane's lesson
with their schoolmates who had not, indicated
further that her former students exhibited mea-
surably less racism.

The scholar "was quite impressed," Jane
says. "As he interpreted his results, my former
students were not only remembering what they
had learned and acting on it, their attitudes
were also rubbing off on their fellow students."

A less welcome indication that the lesson was
not soon forgotten came when Jane introduced
the lesson at the junior high school. She soon
began hearing of complaints by other teachers
about some of her former students. "Through
their participation in the exercise," she ex-
plains, "my students had become extremely

sensitive to discriminatory behavior, and they were often outspoken in their disapproval. When a teacher used the word 'nigger,' for example, it was not unusual for a former student of mine to say, 'If you're going to use that word, I'm going to leave the room.'

"Well, that kind of behavior can come as a shock to a teacher, particularly one who's been talking that way for years. And while I suppose I could be accused of not having taught my students to respect their teachers, I obviously did teach them something about the kind of teachers that deserve respect."

Jane has also had confirmation of the lesson's unexpected effect on learning that she herself had observed. "The very first day I taught the lesson," she recalls, "it seemed to me that students in the so-called 'superior' group were performing academically in ways that would have been impossible for them the day before. I dismissed it as simply my imagination. But the second day, the same thing happened. Children who had been labeled 'inferior' the day before and had been barely able to perform at all were suddenly doing work I would have said was impossible for them."

In the following years, Jane gave her students informal tests in spelling, math, and reading two weeks before the exercise, on each day of the exercise, and again two weeks after it was over. "The results proved that what I had observed was not just my imagination," she says. "Almost without exception, the students' scores went up on the day they were 'superior,' down on the day they were 'inferior,' and then remained on a higher level for the rest of the year after the exercise was over."

In the hope of finding an explanation for this phenomenon, Jane sent some of the tests to experts in the psychology department of Stanford University. "They said the tests seemed to indicate that the children's academic ability was being changed in a twenty-four hour period, which was impossible," she says. Yet the evidence was clear, to Jane at least, that this was precisely what was happening. Eventually, she arrived at her own explanation.

"On the day they are in the 'superior' group and doing genuinely superior work," she says, "they find out for the first time what their true potential is. They learn by actual experience that they can do much better work than they have been doing. Later, when the exercise is over and they continue to work at a higher level, they are simply responding to what they now know they can do.

"It's no longer news in educational circles that children tend to live up—or down—to their teachers' expectations of them," she continues. "In this case, it's the children's expectations of themselves that have changed. Their new expectations are based not on hopes or wishes or even on what their teacher tells them about their abilities, but on their own knowledge and experience. They don't just *think* they can do better work; they *know* they can, because they have."

This discovery, as Jane calls it, has been a surprise bonus of the exercise. "I was really pleased to have learned this," she says. "But I was angry, too, because someone should have told me. Someone should tell all teachers."

The positive results—both expected and un-expected—that Jane could see from her use of the exercise were more than enough to en-courage her to continue it. Yet unanswered, and possibly unanswerable, questions about its long-term effects remained. Then, in 1984, Riceville High School's class of 1979 scheduled a fifth-year reunion. Among the students who had graduated that year were members of her third-grade class of 1970, the students whose lesson in discrimination had been filmed for "The Eye of the Storm." Several of them came to the school to ask Jane if they might see the film again during their reunion. Jane, of course, agreed, and her former third-graders, now young adults, immediately set about con-tacting the rest of the group to urge them to attend both the high school reunion and what they called the "mini-reunion" of their third-grade class.

Their eagerness to have as many of their for-mer classmates as possible at the mini-reunion came as no surprise to Jane. "When you go through this exercise," she says, "the children suffer and the teacher suffers. When it's finally over and you're back together again, there's an intense feeling of love and understanding and empathy that I don't see in my classroom at any other time.

"My third-graders often referred to it as the feeling of being a family, as though the experience had somehow made us all instant cousins. I think that feeling has made the groups of children who have had the lesson different in many ways from their schoolmates who haven't. I know it has affected me. Each time it happens, you catch a tiny glimpse of how society might be if we really believed what we preach about brotherhood, equality, and 'one nation'—and actually practiced it. With this particular class, the fact that what they did was important enough to be filmed for a nationwide television documentary obviously heightened this sense of unity. It made them very special people, both individually and as a group."

Much as Jane looked forward simply to seeing her third-graders of 1970 again, the reunion held prospects of even greater moment for her. This would, after all, be her first opportunity to talk, after the passage of many years, with any of the groups that had been through the exercise. This group, moreover, unlike the others, would be able by watching the film to see through adult eyes exactly how they had responded to the lesson as third-graders. They would not have to depend on their memories.

She wondered, of course, how her former students would react to the film, but she was even more curious to know what they might say about the long-ago lesson itself. Some of them were now married, with children of their own. What would they think of a teacher who put *their* children through such an exercise?

Once she was sure the mini-reunion would actually take place, Jane telephoned to tell me about it. We had kept in touch, and she knew that I had long been fascinated by the idea of somehow tracking down those sixteen third-graders to find out what effect her lesson had had in their lives. "The Eye of the Storm" had, in fact, ended on precisely that note. Standing in front of the Riceville school as children poured past him to board the yellow school buses that would take them home, ABC News correspondent Bill Beutel had said:

Jane Elliott's third-graders have learned something of what it is to be isolated and separated from other people, not because of what you are, but because of the color of your eyes, or the color of a piece of cloth around your neck . . . or the color of your skin.

We don't know if these children will remember what they learned, but it is not likely that they'll forget their courageous and creative teacher, who made their

lives wretched for one day and at the same time gave
them a priceless understanding of human psychology.

We had struggled over that speech, Beutel
and I, both of us impressed with what had happened in Jane Elliott's classroom, both hopeful
that the children *would* somehow remember.
As reporters, however, the most we could do
was raise the question.

Over the years since then, the same question
had occurred to many of the people who saw
"The Eye of the Storm" or read the first edition
of this book. Now, the chance of finding the
answer—and even of capturing it on film for a
new documentary—was irresistible. I quickly
began making arrangements to return to Riceville with a film crew to cover the mini-
reunion.

There was, of course, no way for Jane Elliott
to know in advance how many of the original
sixteen third-graders would actually turn up.
Time had not dealt kindly with all of them.
Russell Ring, the big, good-natured, blue-eyed
boy who had returned from morning recess
soaking wet from wrestling in the snow on the
first day of the exercise, would not be there.
It was Russell whose taunting of John Benttine
had led John to "hit him in the gut," and it
was Russell who had forgotten his glasses on
the second day and who had later swallowed a
pin. Russell's love of wrestling had endured,

and in high school he had won a state wrestling championship. Then, just weeks before graduation, he had been killed in an automobile accident.

John Benttine had also been in a serious automobile accident. He was now a paraplegic. Though several of his classmates had urged him to come, no one knew if he would.

At least six members of that third-grade class had continued their schooling after high school, an impressive showing for students who had originally been assigned to Jane Elliott because of their reading problems and who had often been referred to by both the other third-graders and their teachers that year as "the dummy group." Two of the sixteen, Rex Kozak and Raymond Hansen, had finished college. Rex was now a high school teacher, and Jane knew that he sometimes used "The Eye of the Storm" with his classes. Raymond was working as a paralegal in Chicago. Of all the students in that class, Raymond still stood out in Jane's memory as the one who had seemed to take the most delight in discriminating against his suddenly "inferior" classmates.

Verla Buls, who worked in an office in nearby Cresco, Iowa, was still single. The rest of the girls had married, and all of them had at least one child. One of the three that Jane still thought of as "the inseparables," Sheila Schaefer, was married to a career army man, Tom Flaherty. They were stationed at Fort Campbell, Kentucky. Susan Ginder, the second, had married a man named Gregg Rolland, who was in the air force. They and their three children lived in Fayetteville, North Carolina. The third, Julie Trampel, formerly Julie Smith, was still living in northern Iowa.

Roy Wilson, whose family had left Riceville soon after he completed third grade, was married and living in Sedalia, Missouri, where he worked in a tire factory. Milton Wolthoff, also a factory worker, lived in Rochester, Minnesota. Brian Saltou, whom Jane had always seen as a kind of loner and who was the only one to reject the idea that either group was superior, had served briefly in the navy and was now unemployed. Jane saw him occasionally around town, still very much the loner.

# XI

At nine o'clock on Saturday morning, August 11, 1984, Jane Elliott stood waiting just inside the door of the Riceville school. I was there, too, with a camera crew standing by to film the mini-reunion. Within minutes, eleven of Jane's sixteen former third-graders arrived. John Benttine was not among them.

They had been eight and nine years old when they were in Jane's class; now they were twenty-two and twenty-three. Jane, who had been thirty-seven, was fifty-one. Sandra Dohlman, now Sandra Burke, had brought her husband, Joe. Donna Reddel, now Donna May, brought her baby. The three inseparable girls were there. Julie Trampel came alone. Susan and Gregg Rolland had come all the way from North Carolina, and Sheila and Tom Flaherty from Kentucky. Raymond Hansen was there from Chicago, Milton Wolthoff from Rochester, and Roy Wilson from Sedalia. Rex Kozak and Verla Buls, who lived nearby, also showed up, as did Brian Saltou.

It was an exuberant, happy reunion punctuated by shouted greetings and eager conversational attempts to fill the gap of the intervening years. Bill Beutel and I had been right about one thing: the former students had not forgotten their teacher. "I was surprised at how tall they had grown," Jane says, "and they were amazed at how short I had become." After coffee and doughnuts, everyone went into a classroom to see the film. Since they had all agreed to have their reunion filmed, no one was surprised at the lights we had set up the day before.

The group's first reactions at seeing "The Eye of the Storm" again were pretty much what Jane had anticipated. "They laughed at how they had looked as third-graders and were surprised at how sad they had been when they were in the 'inferior' group," she says. "There was a lot of talking, pointing, and turning around to check each other's reactions. At their request, we ran the film a second time. Then we turned on the lights, put our chairs in a circle, and talked."

Jane turned at once to Raymond Hansen. "Raymond," she said, "I want to know why you were so eager to discriminate against the rest of these kids. At the end of the day, I thought, 'The miserable little Nazi!' Really, I just couldn't stand you." The others laughed and looked at Raymond.

"It felt tremendously evil," Raymond said. "All your inhibitions were gone. And no matter if they were my friends or not, any pent-up hostilities or aggressions that these kids had ever caused you—you had a chance to get it all out."

"And you did it all day," Jane reminded him.

"It became a game," he said. "What new thing can I think of? What new, imaginative thing can I do?"

"Because we had the support of the teacher, and we knew she wasn't going to let anything happen to her special students," another member of that long-ago blue-eyed group added.

Raymond nodded. "I knew I had support. I had the power. I had—you know—prominence in front of the class. If I could come up with a new idea to dig the brown-eyes, I would get your support. I'd get the support of the rest of the blue-eyes."

"What if you hadn't had my support?" Jane asked. "If I had said to you, 'Raymond, turn it off,' what would you have done?"

"It would have been a lot more difficult," Raymond said thoughtfully. "A third-grade child is so tremendously naive and innocent. But you know, I didn't think about anything I was doing or saying—the consequences—what would happen in the future. I was just doing what was fun."

"And you had the okay to go ahead," Jane

said, nodding. Then, turning to Sandra, she said, "I heard you talking to Rex about the collars while we were watching the film."

Sandra, sitting with her husband, nodded. "You hear people talking about, you know, different people—how they're different, and they'd like to have them out of the country—wish they'd go back to Africa—and stuff. And sometimes I just wish I had that collar in my pocket. I could whip it out and put it on them and say, 'Wear this, and put yourself in their place.' I wish they would go through what I went through."

"So that for the rest of your life you'll have that collar in your pocket?" Jane asked.

"Well, not all the time," Sandra said. "I just would like to say, 'You go through what I went through.' "

"But mentally," Jane asked, "you still carry that collar in your pocket?"

"I wish I had the collar in my pocket," Sandra said.

"I think we all carry our collars in our pockets," someone said, and there was a murmur of agreement.

"It's something we're going to carry with us, in our minds, in our feelings, that nobody can ever take away from us," said another.

"Would you like to be able to take it off and never have gone through this?" Jane asked.

Several said no, and the rest agreed.

"Would your lives be easier?" she asked.

Again, their answer was no.

"Is the learning worth the agony?"

There was unanimous agreement that it was. "It made everything a lot different than what it was," said Roy Wilson. "We was a lot better family altogether—even in our houses, we were, probably. Because it was hard on you. When you have your best friend one day, and then he's your enemy the next, it brings it out real quick in you."

"Should every child have the exercise, or should every teacher?" Jane asked.

"Everybody," four or five of them said at once.

"Every school ought to implement something like this program in their early stages of education," Raymond Hansen said, and the group expressed complete agreement.

Jane asked if they remembered the day they were in the "superior" group. "You could do anything. You could read. You could spell. You could do math. The next day, how did you feel?"

"I felt, gee, this stuff was easier yesterday," Sheila said.

"When people say you're dumb, you feel dumb, you act dumb," one of them said. "But when you're on top and you're told you can do no wrong, you can't. You have the classroom in the palm of your hand, and you go."

"You take more chances," said another, "and you're right more often because you take the chance."

"How did you feel when you were in the out-group?" Jane asked.

"Boy, that day, after we went home," Verla Buls said. "Talk about hating somebody. It was there."

"You hated me?" Jane asked.

Verla nodded vigorously. "Yeah. Because of what you were putting us through. Nobody likes to be looked down upon. Nobody likes to be hated, teased, or discriminated against. And it just boggles up inside of you. You just get so mad."

"Were you just angry, or was there more than that?" Jane asked.

Raymond answered. "I felt demoralized. Humiliated."

They talked about the effect the lesson had had in their lives. "When my grandparents start talking about old times," Sheila said, "and they talk about the 'Japs,' I think, how would you like to have been them—the Japanese-Americans—getting thrown into those camps? And I think, calm down and think about it. But when people get older, they're set in their ways, and they're not going to change."

"And when you get older?" Jane asked.

"I'll be set in my ways," Sheila said, "but they're different ways than their ways."

"We're more open-minded, I think," Susan said. "We've got the experience. We went through the lesson, and I think we've got the experience to be a little bit more open-minded."

"Everybody is their own person in their own way, and you can't judge them just by what they do or what they look like," someone added.

"It can't be an 'us' and 'them' situation," someone else said.

"I still find myself sometimes, when I see some blacks together and I see how they act, I think, well, that's black," Susan said. "And right in the next second—I won't even finish the thought—I'm saying, well, I've seen whites do it, I've seen other people do it. It's not just the blacks. It's just that the different color is what hits you first. And then later—as I said, I won't even finish the thought before I remember back when I was in that position."

Another of the women picked up the thought. "If you're with someone who's different from you, you might think, 'Oh, no, I don't want to be near them, because someone may look down on me for associating with that person.' Well, I don't care, because I know what it feels like to be down. I want to be friendly with everybody, because that's the way I want to be treated."

Verla Buls said that though she was still living in a rural area with no blacks, she had met

a number of blacks through friends who had
known them in college or at work. "We was at
a softball game a couple of weekends ago, and
there was this black guy I know. We said, 'Hi,'
and we hugged each other, and some people
really looked, just like, 'What are you doing
with him?' And you just get this burning feeling
in you. You just want to let it out and put them
through what we went through to find out
they're not any different."

Sandra spoke at some length about her son,
who had picked up some anti-black ideas outside the family when Jesse Jackson was running
for president. When he repeated the ideas at
home, she said, "I'd say, 'There's nothing
wrong with him. He's just like you, but he has
a different color.' And my son would just kind
of look at me like, 'What are you talking about,
Mom?' I'm trying—I'm teaching him—"

"It's going to take a while," Brian Saltou said.
"Little kids, they'll listen to a lot of other people, too, so they're going to end up kind of
confused over it."

"But if she keeps on telling him," Jane asked,
"is he going to be the kind of person you kids
are, or is he going to be the kind that judges
people by the color of their skin?"

"Our children won't learn to be prejudiced
from us," Susan said.

Sandra's husband Joe spoke up. "I'm glad
that she's teaching him not to hate, because
even if he does hear this from other people, if

he goes home and he thinks, 'Well, Mom and Dad like the black people, I'm going to like them, too,' I don't think he's going to pick nothing bad up out of it."

Roy Wilson made it clear that for him, at least, the lesson had applications far beyond race. "I live in Missouri," he said, "and a lot of people have punk haircuts. I don't know if they have punk haircuts up here or not. Last year, the high school basketball coach said anybody with a punk haircut couldn't play on the team, and they suspended them. Now is it right because a person's got a different haircut to suspend them from a team?"

Verla Buls (who is tall and slim) made the point that there is also discrimination against fat people. Rex Kozak, who has always been shorter than average, said, "I feel the same kind of emotion I had during the exercise when I see a bunch of bigger kids picking on a kid because he's little."

Raymond Hansen expressed frustration at not being able to convey to others what they had all learned in third grade. "All of us have a special feeling out of this experience," he said, "and sometimes we can share it with other people. But most of the time, I just don't think it sinks in as deeply as it should. I don't think it becomes a part of their moral character like it should."

# XII

After the mini-reunion was over, Jane Elliott talked with me about her impressions of her former students. "They have turned into the kind of people I would have wanted them to be," she said. "I was totally delighted with them. Some of their remarks were exactly the kind of thing I would have wanted them to say."

Jane was, of course, fully aware that the discussion that so pleased her had taken place in a friendly and unthreatening atmosphere among people already in agreement with each other. She also knew that her former students would quite naturally have anticipated her approval of the attitudes they expressed. That left open the question of how they might behave in a hostile environment, with people who didn't agree with their attitudes about race and discrimination. How, for example, would they respond to racist remarks and behavior when they felt alone or outnumbered?

"What I saw and heard was eleven young adults who verbalized strong non-racist attitudes," she said. "They live in a society that, for the most part, tends to approve and reinforce racist and sexist attitudes. What I would hope is that they will be able to say no whenever a racist or sexist remark is made in their presence, to say, 'That's not true,' or at least to ask that such things not be said around them. I would hope that they might do more than just retain the new attitudes they have acquired, that they might actively resist racism and discrimination in one way or another whenever they encounter them.

"But they have to live in the society that exists. And they are undoubtedly going to do whatever they see as necessary to survive in that society. Constantly bucking the system does not win friends and influence people. But even if the exercise did not produce a group of crusaders, I think it has produced a group of young people who, when they encounter racism, will feel at least a twinge of opposition, along with a strong sense that what they are seeing or hearing is simply wrong.

"If I'm right, they are going to have to make a decision at that point. Do I go along, or do I argue? Do I assert myself, or do I just let it go? Or do I join in? At the very least, they're going to be confronted with the need to make a decision. They're going to have to think about it. Without the experience of the exercise, they probably wouldn't be aware that a decision was even called for."

She went back, then, to her original goals. "What I wanted to do was to make those sixteen third-graders aware of their effect on other people. I wanted them to live for one day as other people have to live for a lifetime. And if one day of pain helps them to refuse to inflict that kind of pain on even one other person during their lifetimes, then that one-day exercise was successful for that child.

"I think that has happened. These kids have grown up. Instead of just growing older, they've grown up—more than many of their parents and more than many of their peers. And as they said themselves, the way they feel about people today is because of what happened to them in third grade.

"You always hope that what you teach third-graders will last for at least nine years, until they graduate from high school. This is fourteen years. I never really thought it would last this long. And not only are they remembering it, they are teaching it to their children, which is more than I ever, ever hoped for."

No one who had been in that room—no one who would eventually see the film of the discussion—could doubt that Jane's lesson fourteen years earlier had had a powerful and enduring effect on this group of former students, at least. Crusaders against racism or not, they were clearly young adults who had been inoculated against racist attitudes. Indeed, they seemed to have incorporated into what Raymond Hansen had called their "moral character" an almost automatic opposition to all discrimination based on arbitrary differences.

"I think the reason it has lasted so long and has remained so strong is because it's something that they felt," Jane said. "They internalized this experience. It's something that happened to their insides. It's not a lesson that was simply placed on them from the outside. It's something they experienced.

"I don't know that this kind of deep emotional involvement is something most teachers or school administrators are willing to have happen in their classrooms. It's very risky teaching. I think you could damage a child with this exercise very easily. And I would never suggest that every teacher should use it.

"I think the necessity for the exercise is a crime. I'd like to see the necessity for it wiped out. And I think that if educators were determined enough, we could be instrumental in wiping out the necessity for it. But I want to see something done. I'd like to see this exercise used with all teachers, all administrators. But certainly not with all students, unless it's done by people who are doing it for the right reasons and in the right way."

I asked if she thought that was possible. "I think a group of teachers could be trained to use it properly," she said. "They could go

through the exercise, spend some time analyz-
ing what happened, and then practice doing it
until they were able to do it on their own. They
could learn to do it. If I can do it, most anyone
can do it. It doesn't take a super teacher to do
this exercise."

What it took in Jane Elliott's case was, if not
a super teacher, at least a teacher of a very
special kind. She has always had a way of in-
volving her students, not just in specific subjects, but in the realities behind those subjects.
A study unit on environmental questions, for
example, led one of her classes to a project with
far wider educational implications. A remark
by one third-grader that Riceville didn't have
a park gave rise to a study of parks: their forms
and functions, proper locations, and what they
should contain.

Before long, the class was deeply involved
in everything from landscaping and planting to
the building of walks and benches. They talked
to local businessmen in each of these specialties
about materials, costs, and maintenance. When
they discovered a vacant lot in downtown Riceville that seemed appropriate for a small park,
they did the research necessary to identify its
owner. As it turned out, the property belonged
to the local bank. That discovery led to a meeting of the class with the bank's officers. At each
step, the students were improving their skills
in reading, writing, and mathematics; learning

131

about city planning, competitive bids, private versus public ownership, and, as it turned out, public relations. For the meeting with the bank officers eventually led to the construction of a park where the vacant lot had been.

But Jane Elliott had personal qualities beyond her specific teaching abilities that were unquestionably important to her success with the exercise. She had, first, the uncommon vision to see that a major societal problem—racism—could and should be confronted, not just in the political world of adults, but also, somehow, in the seclusion of a third-grade classroom.

She had the sophistication to distinguish between prejudice and discrimination, to recognize that prejudice is more often the result than the cause of discrimination, and that, odious as it may be, prejudice is by far the less injurious of the two. Prejudices, she saw, serve mostly to restrict the lives of the people who hold them, narrowing their vision and shrinking their worlds. Discrimination, on the other hand, cripples the lives of others—often millions of them. It was in a struggle against discrimination, not prejudice, that Martin Luther King, Jr., had died.

In addition, Jane Elliott had an unusual grasp of the difference between emotional and intellectual education and an intuitive understanding that for schoolchildren to actually experience discrimination, rather than simply to be taught about it, would be likely to make a far deeper impression on them. Finally, she had the creative ability to devise a method by which she might utilize both emotional and intellectual education, in attempting to accomplish her goal.

Still, possessed as she was of all these qualities, something additional was required: the courage to actually teach the lesson. It is one measure of that courage that, among teachers who have learned of the exercise and Jane's use of it, the first question usually asked is, "Was she fired?" The implications of this question are as obvious as they are ominous: public school officials are either intimidated by their fear of community reaction, opposed to innovative teaching, or actually racist—or that is at least the perception of many teachers.

If there has been opposition to her lessons in discrimination on the part of parents or the community at large, Jane is not aware of it. She has, however, been acutely aware of the hostility of a number of her fellow teachers, though she insists that not all of it has been connected with the exercise. "I did lots of strange things in my third-grade classroom, and students generally liked being assigned to my class. They tended to remember what we did and what they learned," she says.

"Well, when you're teaching at the fourth-, fifth-, and sixth-grade levels and some of your students keep saying, 'In Mrs. Elliott's room, we . . .' or 'Mrs. Elliott said . . .,' it can create a problem for some teachers. I'm also not the easiest person in the world to work with. I tend to be more than just a wee bit aggressive. I like to do what I think is best for students, and that doesn't always match the opinions of my peers. So teaching in the same school with me is not always the easiest thing in the world."

As for the exercise itself, Jane has discerned two kinds of negative reactions from some of her fellow teachers. "One, I think, was simple jealousy of the attention I received," she says. "Starting with the local newspaper story, which was picked up by a wire service, which led to my appearance on Johnny Carson's 'Tonight' show, it just seemed to build. When ABC News came to film the exercise, I was again in the local limelight. And when 'The Eye of the Storm' was broadcast, there I was on national television with my whole class. And that, of course, led to even more national publicity. I was interviewed by the press and on other television programs and asked to address a number of professional and educational groups. And I was invited to participate in the 1970 White House Conference on Children and Youth."

When *A Class Divided* was published the following year, Jane and I appeared together on a number of television talk shows. And that, as well as the book itself, led to still more speaking engagements for her.

"It's difficult to see someone else get a lot of attention when she's doing the same job and getting the same pay that you are," Jane says. "The fact that I've had less education than some of my fellow teachers probably didn't help, either. And while it's not particularly pleasant to be the object of resentment and jealousy from your peers, I can live with that and even understand it. What really bothered me was the hostility of some teachers that stemmed, not from jealousy, but from their own racist convictions."

The mere existence of racism in an all-white, all-Christian community like Riceville has seemed to some a strange anomaly. Yet, as students of race relations have long known, no part of the United States—no part of the world—is immune. If even the mildest forms of racial prejudice and discrimination are part of a culture, racism is a natural and perhaps inevitable offspring.

As a college student, Jane Elliott had been dismayed to find racism in her own father, who, she remembered, had been deeply disturbed by Hitler's treatment of Jews. "Racism may seem a strong word to describe his vague, ill-defined anti-Negro prejudices," Jane says now. "He, like most adults in Riceville, simply felt that blacks were inferior. But that, after all, is the essence of racism." Later, renting her house in Waterloo, Iowa, she herself had succumbed to its subtle influence.

Indeed, the very thing that had triggered her first use of the lesson in discrimination embodied a glaring example of this insidious kind of unconscious racism. Watching television in the aftermath of Martin Luther King's assassination, she had been struck not only by the horror of his murder but by the way the news of it was being covered.

"I heard white male newsmen asking black leaders, 'Who is going to hold your people together now? What will they do? Who will control their anger?' " Jane says. "It was as though blacks were subhuman, and someone was going to have to step in and control them. One reporter, referring to the assassination of President Kennedy five years earlier, said, 'When we lost our leader, his widow helped hold us together. Who will hold *them* together?' The separation between 'us' and 'them' could not have been more complete. The attitudes were so arrogant and so condescending that I thought, 'If white male adults react this way, how are my third-graders going to feel?' "

If proof were needed that racist thinking pervaded the atmosphere of all-white Riceville, Iowa, it was provided by the responses of each of Jane Elliott's new third-grade classes when asked, before the lesson began, what they knew about Negroes. Their generally negative answers made it clear that, even at the ages of eight and nine, Riceville children had picked up the cultural cue. And since there were no blacks in the community, and hence no black children in their classrooms, they had had no opportunity for personal experience with blacks that might have led them to question that cue.

Evidence of racism in Riceville's school children points inexorably to its presence in the adult community. It requires no great leap of imagination, then, to anticipate finding racism among teachers drawn from this and similar communities. In fact, Jane had heard racist remarks from fellow Riceville teachers long before she first used her exercise.

Whatever reaction to the lesson she may have anticipated from such teachers, she was unprepared for what actually happened. "It wasn't long before I realized that some teachers were angry about the lesson itself," she says. "I was, after all, attempting to change the status quo. I was teaching that all men are created equal, that racism is irrational and unjust. And here were teachers who simply didn't want children to be taught that blacks are the equals of whites. They didn't believe it themselves, and they didn't want it taught to anyone. Well, that did bother me. And when the attitudes of such teachers began to affect my own children, I was really upset."

Over the years after Jane began her lesson in discrimination, all four of the Elliott children fell victim at one time or another to various kinds of abuse by other students. Like some of her third-graders, they were sometimes called "nigger-lovers." On several occasions, the abuse became physical. "My daughter was pinched, kicked, and spit on in junior high school because her mother was a 'nigger-lover,' " Jane says. "When I reported it to a junior high school teacher and asked what she was going to do about it, she said, 'You should have thought of that before you began this thing. I knew this would happen. Now you'll just have to put up with it.'

"I was appalled. 'That's your response?' I asked. She said, 'That's the way it is.' The principal took the same position.

"For weeks, my seventh-grade son was chased home every night by five teenagers in a car. When they finally caught him, they got out, and two of them beat him up while the others watched. In high school, my daughter's purse and other possessions were destroyed, and the word 'nigger-lover' was written with her own lipstick on the restroom mirror. When I asked the principal what was going to be done about it, he replied that they had no proof that anyone else had actually done it, as though she might have done it herself to get attention.

"The acts of the young people who did these

things were reprehensible. But the response of the teachers and school officials who condoned them was inhuman. Two contradictory lessons were being taught in the Riceville schools. While I was teaching a few children that racism was wrong, some teachers and school administrators were, by their inaction, teaching the exact opposite."

Eventually, the Elliotts moved away from Riceville to a nearby community, where their children finished public school in a different district. Jane, however, continued to teach in the Riceville schools.

# XIII

Some weeks after the mini-reunion of Jane's former third-graders, she was asked to give her lesson in discrimination to a group of adult employees of the Iowa Department of Corrections, the state's prison system. Although I knew she had often conducted the exercise with adults, I had never had a chance to observe, let alone film, one of these adult sessions. Intrigued by her reports of what had happened at a number of them, I decided that this, too, should become a part of the new documentary. With Jane's agreement and the approval of the Corrections Department, I arranged to bring two film crews to Iowa to cover the exercise.

The Iowa Department of Corrections draws its employees from a state with a population that is nearly 98 percent white Anglo-Saxon. Yet while fewer than 3 percent of the people are members of minority groups, minority groups account for more than 20 percent of the state's prisoners. A similar disproportion can be found in other states. In Iowa, one result is that the proportion of minority group members employed to run the prisons is far smaller than the proportion incarcerated in them. It is a situation fraught with potential tensions.

To minimize these tensions, the department has instituted a program aimed at making its overwhelmingly white prison employees sensitive to minority group issues and concerns. It was as a part of this program that Jane Elliott was hired to teach her lesson to a group of the employees. The exercise was scheduled for November 7, 1984, in the conference center of an Iowa City motel, and those chosen to attend were told only that it would be an all-day workshop on human relations. The forty predominantly white men and women who arrived that morning included prison guards, supervisors, probation and parole officers, counselors, instructors, a cook, a maintenance worker, and a prison storekeeper.

"Most of the training we get," one of the men said later, "consists of people giving you information. It wasn't long before I suspected that this was going to be different." One of the first clues came when, in the process of registering and receiving name cards in the entry hall outside the conference room, the group was divided according to eye color. Those with blue eyes were given collars of a particularly

offensive shade of green to pin around their
necks and told to remain in a part of the hall
where there were too few chairs to accom-
modate them. Brown-eyed people were directed to another area, where, in plain sight of
the blue-eyed people, they sat comfortably at
tables with white tablecloths and chatted over
coffee and sweet rolls.

At nine o'clock, when the workshop was
scheduled to begin, the brown-eyed people
were invited to enter the conference room. The
blue-eyed people were told to remain where
they were. Those who tried to use the rest-
rooms found signs on the doors reading
"Browns Only." Those who smoked found the
same signs on the few available ashtrays.

Inside the conference room, chairs had been
arranged in separate front and rear sections.
The front section, where Jane asked the brown-
eyed people to sit, had more than enough
chairs. The rear section, which the blue-eyed
people would occupy, had too few chairs for
their number. Jane quickly prepared the
brown-eyed people for what was going to happen. "This is not something I can do alone,"
she said finally. "This exercise won't work without your cooperation. The blue-eyed people
will be joining us soon, and we have some rules
that apply only to them. Blue-eyed people are
not allowed to sit in these empty chairs in the
front of the room. Do not let a blue-eyed person sit next to you. You know you can't trust

them, and besides, they don't smell good. Everybody knows that about blue-eyed people. You don't know what you might catch from a blue-eyed person."

She asked them to think of experiences they might have had that would illustrate the inferiority of blue-eyed people. The brown-eyed group, which of course included the handful of blacks who had come to the workshop, caught on quickly to its intended role in the exercise.

By 9:20, the blue-eyed people, still waiting in the entry hall, were visibly annoyed. One man suggested that they simply barge into the conference room uninvited. Another thought they should leave and go home. No one budged. A woman said, "Nobody seems to have the courage of his convictions. We're all doing a lot of talking, but nobody takes any action." A second woman said, "Suppose we all sing real loud?" A man suggested "We Shall Overcome," and while that brought laughter, no one sang.

When the blue-eyed people were at last told to enter the room, they were instructed to leave their coats and purses on the floor in a corner at the back. The brown-eyed people, comfortably settled in the front of the room, had their coats, purses, and briefcases with them.

As they looked for places to sit, the blue-eyed people noticed signs that had been hung on the walls. One read: "If I have but one life

to live, let me live it as a brown-eyed person."
Another asked: "Would you want your sister
to marry a blue-eye?" Still another read: "I'm
not prejudiced; some of my best friends are
blue-eyed."

When the chairs in the rear had been filled
and blue-eyed people began drifting toward
the front of the room, Jane made it clear that
the front section was for brown-eyed people
only. One blue-eyed man tried to move an
empty chair to the back. He was told to leave
it where it was, and he did. Eventually, a number of blue-eyed people were forced to stand
or sit on the floor in the back.

When the room was quiet, Jane said to the
blue-eyed people, "It would be to your advantage in the future if you'd get to meetings on
time." For all their annoyance at being kept
waiting in the hall, there was no response.
When she noticed that an attractive, well-
dressed blue-eyed woman was chewing gum,
Jane said to her, "It would also be to *your*
advantage if you'd put your gum away."

"I'll leave," the woman said flippantly.

"Put your gum away," Jane repeated.

"I'll leave," the woman said again, this time
with just a trace of derision.

"Do you want to get paid for today?" Jane
asked.

The woman nodded.

"Then stay, but put your gum away."

"I don't have a purse," the woman explained

145

with elaborate patience, "so I don't have any place to put my gum."

"I'm sure you're inventive enough to find a place for your gum," Jane said.

At that, the woman took the gum from her mouth and stuck it defiantly on the bottom of her chair. Jane watched quietly and then said to the brown-eyed people in the front of the room, "I'd like for you to notice where she put her gum." The brown-eyed people, who had watched the entire exchange, had noticed.

"You have this problem with blue-eyed people," Jane told them. "You give them something decent, and they just wreck it." She paused to let that sink in. "You'll also notice that blue-eyed people spend a lot of time playing 'Look at me. See how cute I am. I can be funny. I can make a joke of this. This is amusing. I'm amused by this.'

"Another thing that is obvious about blue-eyed people is that they are poor listeners," she continued, and she began dictating what she called the "listening skills" for the entire group to write down. The first was, "Good listeners have quiet hands, feet, and mouths."

A blue-eyed man in the back, lounging against the wall, eyes on the ceiling, caught her attention. "I'd like for you to look at the man in the back in the black jacket," she said. There was a rustle of movement as everyone turned to look. "The game we're playing is 'playing it cool,' " she continued. " 'Nobody can

146

bother me, man. I can handle this. I don't have to do this. I'm gonna ignore this whole thing.' "

The man in the black jacket looked at Jane, then quickly away, and finally at the floor, running a hand down the length of his face in a gesture of bored annoyance.

As the brown-eyed people busily took down the four listening skills Jane dictated, it quickly became apparent that many of the blue-eyed people were not writing. Challenged by Jane, several said they had left their pens or pencils in their coats or purses in the back of the room. Jane suggested they share the pencils they had.

When the man in the black jacket made no effort to borrow a pencil, Jane singled him out again. "Sir," she said. "I realize that you feel you don't need to write this down, but whether or not you write it down, perhaps you could remember it."

"I'll borrow a pen," he said.

"Good listeners have quiet hands, feet, and mouths," Jane repeated. "Do you know what that means?"

Now clearly rattled, he replied, "I'm not sure."

"I believe that," Jane said. "Do you want me to explain it to you?"

"That's okay," he said. "I'll get a pencil and write this down directly."

"Look, blue-eyed people," Jane said to those around him. "Many of you have pencils. Will one of you please lend him a pencil? Or don't you trust him? Which I can understand." Then, turning to the brown-eyed people, she asked, "In the last ten minutes, what have you observed about blue-eyed people?"

A tall, good-looking black man spoke up. "Blue-eyed people are very stubborn, very self-centered, and wish to control as much of their surroundings as possible—people-wise, I mean. Very inconsiderate people. I don't even know why you have them here in the first place."

"We have them here because we are required to have them here," Jane replied.

"We have to, eh?"

"This is one of the things you have to put up with," she added.

As the exercise went on and Jane continued to treat blue-eyed people as inferiors, other brown-eyed men and women joined in. A brown-eyed white woman spoke of her two nephews, one blue-eyed, the other brown-eyed. "The blue-eyed one, he never cleans his room, and he's real lazy. He doesn't seem to have a lot of energy. But the brown-eyed one, he's real outgoing, and he plays in sports, and he's pretty good at it. He just seems like a better kid. So if I have kids, I hope they have brown eyes."

"Are you married?" Jane asked.

"No."

"Then, it's a good thing you don't have kids, isn't it?"

"Right," the woman replied.

"But you will know what to do when you choose a mate."

"Right," she said again.

When Jane had finished dictating the listening skills, she asked the man in the black jacket, whom someone had referred to as Roger, to read the first one to her.

"I haven't got it on my paper yet," he said.

"Oh, why is that?" Jane asked.

"I haven't borrowed the pencil to write it down as yet."

"And you think it's unnecessary?"

Roger had clearly had enough of this. "Well, at this particular point, yes, I do," he said with obvious annoyance.

"Why?" Jane asked.

Most of the people in the room had turned to look at him again. He shook his head, apparently at a loss for an answer. Finally, he said, "Well, I have it in my head for the most part."

But Jane was not about to let up. "There's a lot of space up there for it, isn't there, friend?" she said. "Do you suppose you could tell me what it is?"

"It has something to do with keeping your hands and feet still, as I recall."

"It has something to do with that," Jane repeated. When this brought laughter from some of the blue-eyed people, she turned quickly to them. "I find it interesting that you're amused by our having to stand here and wait for this man to do something that everybody else has already done. I find that highly interesting. Stupid, but interesting." Then, turning once more to the brown-eyed group, she asked, "If you are in a situation where someone is constantly refusing to do what the people in authority ask them to do, what do you know about that person?"

"I think it's a game with them," a brown-eyed white man in a business suit volunteered. "Attention."

"Has it gained anything for this gentleman?" Jane asked.

"Disrespect from, I think, the brown-eyed people," he replied.

"Has it proven anything to the brown-eyed people?"

"Yes," the man said. "That this is a typical trait of a blue-eyed person."

Turning once more to Roger, Jane said, "Now read the second listening skill."

"I don't have the second one," Roger said.

"You don't have the second one either?"

"No."

"You were keeping it in your head," Jane reminded him. "What happened to that plan?"

"Just the first one I had in my head," Roger said. "Not the second one."

"Oh. The other three aren't important?"

"Well, they're probably important," Roger admitted grudgingly.

"But not important enough for you to write down, right?"

"Well," Roger said, "they're important. I should've written them down, most probably."

"Most probably?" Jane mimicked. Turning again to the brown-eyed people, she asked, "What do you know now about blue-eyed people that you didn't know before?"

A black man responded. "I'm finding I'm going to have to explain things a bit more explicitly to a blue-eyed person than I would to a brown-eyed person."

"How many times did I have to repeat the listening skills for Roger?" she asked.

The man turned to look at Roger. "Well, brother Roger is having a rough time today, isn't he? It was about six or seven different times."

Later, Jane handed out a written test deliberately biased in favor of American blacks. To assure that the entire brown-eyed group did well on it, she had given them half of the correct answers before the blue-eyed people entered the room. When the test was over, she asked the brown-eyed people to correct all the papers and report the scores. Not surprisingly, the brown-eyed people all got very good scores. It was during the process of reporting the scores that Jane had her second confrontation with the woman who had earlier been chewing gum.

A brown-eyed man reported a score of only eleven correct answers on a test paper identified only by the initials "K. R."

"K. R.?" Jane asked. "Just an initial? No last name?"

"No names," the man said. At that, the blue-eyed woman who had been chewing gum stood up to claim the paper. When the brown-eyed man had trouble reading the name of another blue-eyed woman, she identified herself and took her test paper from him. Then a brown-eyed woman reported the score of a paper signed only "E. Riley." E. Riley turned out to be a blue-eyed woman sitting with the previous two.

"You know," Jane said to the three of them, "what you do to the image of blues with your behavior is unfortunate. What you three people do to the image of women with your behavior really makes me angry. The fact that you do this kind of sloppy work reflects badly on women. I resent that doubly."

K. R. leaned forward. "Ma'am," she said with a transparent pretense of civility, "I'd really appreciate it if you'd call us by name. When you say 'you three people,' we don't know who you are speaking to. It could be anyone here."

"My dear," Jane replied, echoing her mock

deference, "if you wanted me to call you by name, you'd have put your name on your paper."

"It's on my coat," K. R. said, holding up the name card on the lapel of her suit jacket.

"It was to be on your paper," Jane said.

"You didn't see my paper, ma'am."

"I didn't get your name, either, because it wasn't on your paper," Jane replied.

"That's right."

"All right," Jane said. "Now how could one call you by your name if you don't care enough about your name to put it on your paper?"

"You can't even read?" K. R. asked sarcastically, pointing again to her name card.

"Don't expect me to worry about it if you don't put it on your paper. Don't sit there and say, 'My name is important to me,' after you have just deliberately *not* put it on your paper."

"I don't remember saying my name was important to me," K. R. said icily. "I remember saying I'd like to know who you're speaking to when you say, 'you three.'"

"Then what should you do?" Jane asked.

"Ask that you use my name, which I did."

"And where should your name have been?"

"Right here where it is," K. R. said, holding up her name card once more. "And on my birth certificate."

"Is it on your paper?" Jane asked.

"No, ma'am."

"Where'd you get a birth certificate?"

K. R. hesitated only an instant. "Out of a slot machine," she snapped. "Same as you did, lady."

"I think you're probably right about your own," Jane said.

"At least I know who my parents are, ma'am," K. R. said angrily.

Addressing an Oriental man in the brown-eyed group, Jane asked, "Is she being rude?"

"Yes," he said.

"Is she being inconsiderate?"

"Yes."

"Is she being uncooperative?"

"Yes."

"Is she being insulting?"

"Yes."

"Are all those the things we've accused blue-eyed people of being?"

"Yes."

"Is she proving that we're right?"

"Yes."

Encouraged, perhaps, by K. R.'s defiance, a blue-eyed man spoke up. "Do you feel that there are important blue-eyed people?"

"There are exceptions to every rule," Jane replied.

"And what are those exceptions?" he persisted.

"There are a few important blue-eyed people," she answered.

"Do you think that you are one of them?" a blue-eyed woman asked.

"No," Jane said immediately.

"Then why are you up there?" asked the man who had first raised the question.

"I'm blue-eyed," Jane said. "The difference between you and me is, I have a brown-eyed husband and brown-eyed offspring, and I've learned how to behave in a brown-eyed society. And when you can act brown enough, then you, too, can be where I am."

That was apparently too much for K. R. "I wouldn't want to be where you are," she said.

"Are you certain?" asked Jane.

"Absolutely positive."

"You like where you are?"

"I love where I am."

"You like it so much that you don't even identify yourself on your paper," Jane said.

"I don't need to, lady," K. R. snapped.

It was the second time K. R. had called her "lady," and this time Jane took notice of it. Turning to the brown-eyed group, she asked, "Her using the term 'lady' where I'm concerned—what do you think she's trying to do? Is it ignorance, or is it deliberately insulting?"

A brown-eyed woman said, "I would say it was deliberately insulting."

"If it's ignorance," Jane said, "she needs to be taught that to many of us the word 'lady' is a pejorative. I don't appreciate it. It's a put-down. And it's used to keep women in their place."

"I will call you by the correct name after

155

this," K. R. promised. "I won't be kind."

"That was kindness on your part?" Jane asked with obvious disbelief.

"Yes," K. R. replied. "I think to call someone a lady is a kindness."

"Then your problem *is* ignorance."

"You can call me 'lady' any time you like," K. R. said.

"I wouldn't do that to you."

"No, I know you wouldn't."

"I really wouldn't," Jane said. "And that's part of the problem—a total lack of awareness of what sexism amounts to, and how much you contribute to the sexism that keeps you where you are."

"I like where I am, lady," K. R. fired back, and then, realizing what she had said, she grinned and said, "I did it again, didn't I?"

The blue-eyed man who had tried to take a chair from the front of the room at the beginning of the session now spoke up for the first time. "I'm getting kind of fed up with this whole bunch of garbage," he said.

"Why?" asked Jane.

"Brown-eyed people are no different than we are," he said. "I hate to tell them that. They have these false delusions and such."

"Are they being disruptive?" Jane asked.

"No," he conceded. "You trained them very well. I think that's what they did with the storm troopers in Germany also." And then, addressing the brown-eyed people in the front of the room, "You guys do a real good job sitting up there."

"You think that what's happening here today feels the way it would have felt to be in Nazi Germany?" she asked.

"Yes," he replied.

"If we're in Nazi Germany, who are you?" Jane asked, gesturing at the blue-eyed group.

"The Jews," he said.

Jane had long ago decided that with adult groups there was neither the time nor the need to reverse the groups as she did with school-children, and, after a lunch break, she announced to the Corrections Department employees that the first part of the workshop was over. "Let's talk about what happened this morning," she suggested. The tension that had gripped the room disappeared, and within minutes one after another of the blue-eyed people was struggling to describe how the experience had felt—and why.

"Did you learn anything this morning?" Jane asked Roger.

Roger, who had shed his black jacket, was now in the front of the room. "I think I learned from the experience a feeling like I was in a glass cage, and I was powerless. There was a sense of hopelessness. I was angry. I wanted to speak up, and yet I knew if I spoke up I'd be attacked. I had a sense of hopelessness, depression."

"Had you experienced that before?" Jane asked him.

"I realized this morning that there were very few times in my life that I've ever been discriminated against. Very few."

"And you were this uncomfortable in an hour and a half?"

"I was amazed at how uncomfortable I was in the first fifteen minutes," Roger said.

"Can you empathize at all with blacks, minority group members, in this country?"

"I'm hoping better than before," he said.

David Stokesbury, the blue-eyed man who had drawn the analogy with Nazi Germany, said, "If we tried to argue with you, you would use just the mere argument as reason for us being lesser than the brown-eyed folks. You know, you couldn't win."

"Yes, but don't we do that every day?" Jane asked.

"I think some do, yeah," he admitted, "but I would hope that I never get so unreasonable. You know, the statements you were making were groundless, and yet we couldn't argue with them, because if we argued, then we were argumentative and—you know—not listening and getting out of our place and all that stuff. And that was frustrating to me. And also frustrating to me was the other blue-eyed people who were sitting on their hands. My group here was, I don't think, boisterous enough in opposition to the whole thing."

Jane nodded. "Why didn't you people support one another?" she asked. "The blue-eyed people on this side," she said, indicating one half of the room, "just sat there. And let's face it, you covered your asses. Right? Why did you just sit there?"

A blue-eyed man who had done just that said, "I think that's symptomatic of the problem as a whole. We see that, you know, in society in general. We see a few people who are making a lot of noise and the rest of the people sitting back waiting to see what they're going to do."

"As long as I was picking on him," Jane said, "I was leaving you alone. Right?"

"Right."

"I'd say a lot of people do that," a blue-eyed woman said. "They let a few people do their fighting for them, and they stand back and, if this person's going to win, then they'll get on his side. But if that person's not going to win, they'll stay back over here, you know. That's just how it works."

Turning back to the man, Jane asked, "If you were in a real situation where you had to do something about racism, would you stand up and be counted?"

"*What* I would do, I don't know," he said. "It would depend on the exigencies."

"But you would do something?"

"I would *have* to do something. I couldn't go home tonight and face my kids if I didn't."

159

Turning to the other group, Jane asked, "How did you brown-eyed people feel while this was going on?"

"I had a sense of relief that I wasn't a blue-eyed person," a man said immediately.

Jane nodded. "A sense of relief that you had the right color eyes."

"Right."

"Absolutely," Jane said.

The blue-eyed man who had asked if there were any important blue-eyed people said, "I really understood—at least I felt that I understood—what it was like to be in the minority."

K. R. had not yet spoken. "Why were you angry?" Jane asked her.

"First of all," she said, "because it was unreasonable. Secondly, because I felt discriminated against. Thirdly, I think that all of us—everyone in this room—has dealt with discrimination on both sides. You don't have to be black or Jewish or Mexican or anything to have felt discrimination in your life. And as you become an adult, you learn to deal with those feelings within yourself, and you learn to handle those. And when you feel yourself in a situation that you can't get out of, which we couldn't—we were a captive audience, and it was not a normal situation, because normally you aren't badgered . . ." She stopped, perhaps realizing that she was describing precisely the normal situation of many blacks.

"What if you had to spend the rest of your

life this way?" Jane asked her.

K. R. shook her head. "I don't know how to answer that," she admitted.

But a black woman in the brown-eyed group did. Speaking directly to K. R., she said, "You don't wake up every morning knowing that you're different. You wake up as a white woman, who is going to her job at eight o'clock or whatever. Where a black person is going to wake up knowing, from the minute they get out of the bed and look in the mirror, they're black, and they have to deal with the problems they've had to deal with ever since they were young—and realize that 'I am different, and I have to deal with life differently. Things are different for me.'

"And I don't think you can really say that you have felt—maybe you have felt some sort of discrimination—but you haven't felt what it is like for a black woman: to go through the daily experience of arguing and saying, 'Listen to me. My point of view is good, you know. What I have to offer here is good.' And no one wants to listen, because white is right. That's the way things are."

K. R. had listened intently, and when the black woman stopped, she nodded her agreement.

When the discussion was over, Jane spoke briefly about teaching the same lesson to schoolchildren. To illustrate, she ran "The Eye of the Storm" for them. That elicited still more questions and discussion. When she finally declared the workshop over, many of the Corrections Department employees lingered to talk some more. A number of them made it a point to thank Jane for the experience.

# XIV

As involved as I was in the filming of the workshop, I found it impossible not to be caught up
in the drama that was taking place before our
cameras. Jane had previously given the lesson
to more than seventy adult groups, most of
them composed of teachers, and though each
experience had been unique, she had concluded that adults generally reacted to it in
much the same way as schoolchildren. What I
saw convinced me that she was right. The blue-
eyed Corrections Department employees had
exhibited all of the hopelessness, withdrawal,
and frustration—and even more of the anger—
that I had first seen and filmed fourteen years
earlier in Jane's third-grade classroom. And
when the exercise was over, the adults had
come to many of the same conclusions the
third-graders had drawn.

Unlike the third-graders, however, the supposedly inferior adults never appeared to forget

that what was happening was simply an exercise. Not for a moment did they actually believe that they were inferior. Yet they became every bit as entangled in the web of Jane's artificial scheme of discrimination as if it had been real. No matter what they said or did, it was somehow used as proof of their inferiority. As David Stokesbury had said, "You couldn't win."

Later, screening the film of the exercise in an editing room, where I could look at various segments again and again, the similarities of what had happened in that room to the reality of discrimination in America literally jumped out at me. The reactions of the blue-eyed men and women to the dilemma in which Jane had placed them so accurately reflected the reactions of American blacks and other minority group members that the conference room had truly become a microcosm of a racist society. Everywhere I looked in the film there were mirror images of the real world.

Most of the blue-eyed people, for example, had not only remained silent, as Stokesbury had complained, they had done nothing that might call attention to themselves. Their demeanor was that of people clearly hoping not to be noticed, like students desperately wishing not to be called on in a class. Each in his own way, all of them were trying to blend anonymously into the larger group.

Even Stokesbury, who eventually charged

Jane with having trained the brown-eyed people to behave like storm troopers, had remained silent for most of the session. Leaning
against the wall beside Roger during Roger's
long ordeal, he had made no effort to inter-
vene. And all of this evasive behavior had been
foreshadowed by the remark of a blue-eyed
woman in the hall outside the conference room
before the exercise began. "Nobody seems to
have the courage of his convictions," she had
said. "We're all doing a lot of talking, but nobody takes any action."

K. R. had been the first to resist, but even
she had done so only when provoked by Jane's
request that she put her gum away. Her ulti-
mate response—putting her gum on the bottom of her chair—had been the first small act
of defiance.

Roger, as the film made unmistakably clear,
had indeed been "playing it cool" when Jane
first noticed him, and that, too, had been a
silent expression of disdain, dictated, perhaps,
by a need to retain his self-esteem in the face
of unwarranted discrimination that he dared
not oppose outright.

Later, under continuous pressure, Roger
had tried various tactics to escape Jane's attention. None of them worked. Still later, describing how it had felt, he put his sense of isolation
and defeat into words that must have echoed
the experiences of many blacks. He had, he
said, experienced "a feeling like I was in a glass

cage, and I was powerless. I was angry. I wanted to speak up, and yet I knew if I spoke up, I'd be attacked."

Studying the film, I saw also that until David Stokesbury had declared himself "fed up with this whole bunch of garbage" no one had really attacked the premise of the discrimination: that brown-eyed people were superior to blue-eyed people. Stokesbury had finally stated it baldly: "Brown-eyed people are no different than we are."

Before that, all opposition had taken the form of a defense against personal attack: K. R.'s putting her gum under her chair, Roger's annoyed declaration that he felt it unnecessary to write down the listening skills, K. R.'s objection to Jane's reference to her as one of "you three people." Even the questions about the existence of important blue-eyed people and whether Jane considered herself one of them— while they pinpointed eye color as the basis of the discrimination—were too feeble to be characterized as attacks on the underlying premise of the exercise.

I noticed another intriguing fact. None of the blue-eyed people had responded at all to the discriminatory statements of the brown-eyed people. What little opposition there had been had been aimed at Jane. Only at the end— when David Stokesbury had said of the brown-eyed members of the group that "they have these false delusions and such"—was the fact that they had cooperated in the discrimination even mentioned. It was almost as if by ignoring the complicity of the brown-eyed people in the discrimination against them, they could pretend, to themselves at least, that their problem consisted solely in the behavior of a single irrational individual in a position of authority.

Roger's description of feeling "like I was in a glass cage" brought immediately to mind the fact that many victims of racial discrimination are easily identifiable by color or other physical characteristics. They cannot escape standing out in a crowd. They know, as the black woman said later, "from the moment they get out of bed and look in the mirror" that they are different and have to deal with life differently. Hence, Roger's feeling of being powerless to change things, his sense of hopelessness.

Nor is difference, identifiable or not, the significant factor. "Being different," as Jane Elliott later pointed out, "is not the problem. The problem is majority group reaction to differentness. As long as members of the majority group see differences as negative and respond in negative ways to those who possess them, the problems of racism and sexism and ageism will persist. Just as the acceptance of the blue-eyed people in that room should not have depended on their ability to act like the brown-eyed people, so the acceptance of minority group members in this society should not depend on their ability to act white, nor that of females on their ability to act male, nor that of old people on their ability to look or act young."

David Stokesbury's complaint that argument against Jane's assertions of blue-eyed inferiority was used as further proof of inferiority was a reminder of how often the results of discrimination are cited as proof of the validity of prejudice. As Jane had said years earlier, "It's a simple enough equation: choose a group, discriminate against it, force it by your discrimination to look and act inferior, and then point to the way it looks and acts as proof of its inferiority." It was the irrationality of this way of thinking that caused Stokesbury's feelings of frustration and his statement, "You couldn't win."

There was even something revealing in the statement of one blue-eyed man that, in a real situation of racism, he would have to take a stand or he couldn't face his children. Wasn't he saying, in effect, that children, who have had little opportunity to contribute actively to racism, are more likely than adults to sense that it is wrong? Or that children, more than adults, are uncomfortable in a world in which simple fairness is not the rule?

K. R. had stated her belief that everyone—not just members of specific minority groups—experienced discrimination, and that as you became an adult, you learned to handle it. Wasn't that akin to saying that if other groups had overcome handicaps, why couldn't these?

What she specifically complained of was not so much the discrimination as being in what she described as a captive audience and being badgered. But as the black woman who answered her pointed out indirectly, weren't blacks in a captive audience and badgered by discrimination every day of their lives?

Jane saw something more. "K. R. seemed also to be saying that there is something in minority group members that makes it impossible for them to 'grow up' and 'handle' their reactions to discrimination in an adult fashion—as she has. She seemed to forget that when she was put in a situation similar to what minority groups experience every day, she was unable to 'handle it' for even two hours. Instead, she reacted exactly as she has undoubtedly seen members of minority groups react.

"She might well have concluded from her own feelings and behavior that the way minority group members react to discrimination is not the result of some weakness in their genes but simply the way human beings react to being treated unfairly because of something over which they have no control by people unable—or unwilling—to admit that *they* have a problem in dealing with those who are different from them."

Although few of these points had come up explicitly in the discussion that followed the exercise, it was clear from what had been said that a good deal of learning had taken place. Yet, as had been the case with Jane Elliott's third-graders in 1970, there was no easy way of knowing how long it would last.

As the members of my two film crews went about taking down their lights and packing up their equipment after the session, they talked of little else than what they had seen and heard. Some of them had been with me when we filmed the mini-reunion in Riceville three months earlier, and they had become friendly with Jane and her family during the times when we were not filming. And while all of them had noted her behavior with the third-graders in "The Eye of the Storm," they were still astonished at her ability to transform herself from the warm and witty woman they knew into the uncompromising bigot they saw that morning. More than one of them told me later that his attitudes, too, had been changed by the experience.

The new hour-long documentary was called "A Class Divided," after the first edition of this book. The first half of the film, which dealt with the mini-reunion of Jane's third-grade class of 1970, included scenes from the earlier documentary, "The Eye of the Storm." The second half was devoted to Jane's use of the exercise with the employees of the Iowa Department of Corrections.

Broadcast on March 26, 1985, on the PBS series *Frontline,* the program later received an Emmy and a number of other awards. Before the broadcast, it had been hailed by one reviewer as "a riveting, and potentially life-changing, hour." Ironically, among those whose lives it changed was Jane Elliott.

Within weeks of the broadcast she began receiving requests from organizations to teach her lesson to groups of their employees. At first, she accepted only those she could somehow fit into her teaching schedule. As the demand increased, however, it became clear that she would have to make a choice between teaching in or out of the classroom. Past attempts to do both had led to opposition to adjustments in her teaching schedule by the local chapter of the National Education Association, which represented Riceville's teachers, and a subsequent confrontation between the association and the school administration. In 1986, to avoid yet another such contest, Jane left the Riceville schools to take up a new career. Today, her success in teaching the lesson to employees of a growing number of organizations has served only to increase the demand for her services, and she is currently planning to train a number of others to carry out the exercise under her supervision.

Meanwhile, demand for the film and video cassettes of "A Class Divided" has equaled the earlier demand for "The Eye of the Storm."

Like its predecessor, it has become a best-seller in educational distribution.

What began in 1968 in a third-grade classroom has since spread in ever-widening circles. The mini-reunion of Jane Elliott's 1970 students, documented in "A Class Divided," brought proof that her two-day lesson in discrimination had significantly changed their lives. These were young adults who clearly had been inoculated against racism—and every other kind of invidious discrimination.

What Jane Elliott has done is to me no less significant than what Jonas Salk did with his polio vaccine in the 1950s. No longer need children's bodies be crippled by polio. Now we can prevent the crippling of their minds by racism. A teacher has shown us how. The only remaining question is whether we will *apply* the treatment—which consists, like the vaccine, of a tiny dose of the disease.